# CHRONICLES OF AN
# Irreverent
# Reverend

CHRONICLES OF AN

# Irreverent
# Reverend

*what goes wrong
can make you better*

*Joe*

DR A. ~~JOSEPH BAROODY JR~~.

CHRONICLES OF AN IRREVERENT REVEREND:
What Goes Wrong Can Make You Better

Copyright © 2013 by A. Joseph Baroody Jr.
ISBN: 978-0-9841073-8-4

Printed in the United States of America
First Edition

Published by Joggling Board Press

Joggling Board Press LLC
PO Box 13029
Charleston, SC 29422

JogglingBoardpress
*Books—In the Spirit of the South*

www.jogglingboardpress.com

Joggling Board Press books may be purchased for educational, business or sales promotional use.

For information, please contact sales@jogglingboardpress.com.

Library of Congress Cataloging in Publication Data applied for

Book design by Torborg Davern
Interior design by Shanna McGarry
Author photo by Jackie McLean

# Acknowledgments

This is my first book. Writing it became a lesson in what it means to string words and ideas together in a way that inspires and gives meaning. My teachers in this endeavor have been Susan Kammeraad-Campbell and Russ McCollom, the editors at Joggling Board Press. Through all the editing, the jostling back and forth, the rewrites, the long hours and the late nights, they have been great teachers and colleagues. Even better, they have become caring and trusted friends. I thank them for the journey.

I am also grateful to the rest of the Joggling Board Press team – Will Green, Katelyn Harrell, Emily Li, Shanna McGarry and Tom Smith. This book would never have happened without their insight and dedication.

And a special thanks to Missy Brown for typing much of the manuscript, and especially for her insights and helpful suggestions. God has a special place reserved for English teachers.

In this book you, Reader, will meet my family, friends and those I've been privileged to encounter in my career as an irreverent Reverend. May they forgive me for any liberties I have taken that might test their modesty or patience. Most of all, my hope is that you will meet me, and in meeting me, find that it's okay to make mistakes, to bend the rules, to fall flat on your face and quite possibly come through it all not just okay, but better than you were before.

*Joe*

## Dedication

To Mac and Blakely, my dear children: I love you with all my heart. Send Dad some money.

To Carson and James Wyatt, my wonderful grandchildren. You have brought great joy to Joe-Joe's life. Tell your mom and Uncle Mac to send money.

And especially to my wife Nancy: Sometimes I forget to say how thankful I am that God's gentle hand led you my way.

# Contents

# 1

## *Chocolate Naked Ladies*

The two ladies dressed in formal evening gowns led us up a grand spiral staircase to a large bedroom. No ordinary brothel was this. No sir. My buddy and I had the foresight and good taste to begin our tour of Europe by entering a Parisian house of ill repute. The French prostitutes – two of the most beautiful women my nineteen-year-old eyes had ever gazed upon – were angels leading us up the stairway to heaven.

Entrance to heaven requires baptism. And so the two angels removed our shoes, unbuckled our pants, lowered our Fruits of the Loom, and purified us with soap and water. With our pants bunched around our ankles they quickly shuffled us to two chairs placed at the foot of a large, elegant bed covered in light blue silk sheets. Sitting on a table between the chairs was a bowl filled with chocolate miniature naked ladies.

The two prostitutes shed their evening gowns, slid onto the silk sheets, and performed for us. Ten minutes and several chocolate ladies later, my friend left with his escort while mine smoothed the silk sheets and beckoned me to her. With lips smeared in chocolate, and my pants still twisted around my ankles, I eagerly responded.

The deal was thirty dollars for thirty minutes of ecstasy. My thirty minutes, however, lasted about three.

Frustrated, I handed her a fifty dollar travelers' check and waited for the change. When the change did not appear, I made a polite query about it. In return, I received a barrage of loud clacking in French. The only words remotely familiar to me were *"Oui Oui,"* which, in the heat of the moment, I took as some sort of slur about my anatomy.

I slowly descended the spiral staircase, head down, studying my feet. In the first few hours of my first night in Europe, I had managed to lose fifty of the three hundred dollars my father had allowed me for spending money, not to mention what little dignity I possessed. May as well get it over with, I thought. I found a phone booth and placed the dreaded call. Daddy chastised me with a quote from Proverbs 5:20: *And why wilt thou, my son, be ravished with a strange woman, and embrace the bosom of a stranger?* I hesitated to tell him that the only bosoms I had actually embraced were those belonging to the little chocolate ladies.

I took a seat at a table to wait on my friend who undoubtedly was more skilled at locating the correct bosoms. A waiter told me I must order a drink if I wanted to sit at a table. I ordered a Coke. A buck twenty-five. Great.

While drowning my sorrows in my drink, the chair beside me slid out. Expecting to see my friend, I froze as one of the women I had seen in the house took a seat. She looked ravishing in her evening gown, and she spoke in English. "One of my friends heard you talking on the phone." Apparently they all knew English. "I thought you could use some of these." She handed me a square white box. The Brothel's logo was inscribed on the top. Classy.

I opened the box, took out one of the chocolate naked ladies, and bit into it. She smiled, gently patted my hand, and disappeared into the night. My buddy arrived, and we took a taxi back to the hotel. We ate more naked ladies while he bragged about his escapade.

In my room I fished around for the few remaining ladies. That's when I noticed it. Folded neatly in the bottom of the box was my fifty dollar travelers' check. I fell asleep holding the box, my lips smeared in chocolate.

# 2

## *Bubba, Childbirth and the Power of Prayer*

The head nurse of the maternity floor was Marge "The Sarge" Hickson, a Vietnam vet. She was scary-smart and hard as nails. She had seen it all. Not much impressed the Sarge; I certainly didn't. Our first meeting was brief and formal. I introduced myself as the floor's new chaplain but didn't mention I was new to this maternity stuff.

"That's fine," she said. "Let me know if you need anything."

That was it.

Every chaplain intern has teachable moments – those remarkable experiences that reveal life's deeper meanings. Mine came three weeks after meeting the Sarge. As I approached room 425, where the patient was scheduled for a cesarean section the next morning, I heard a series of loud, shrill cries piercing the air. According to my theology, cries like that coming from a pregnant woman meant God was telling me He didn't want me to be there and I was to leave the area as quickly as possible. Ever obedient to God's will, I about-faced. Halfway through a quick exit, a vise-like grip took my arm and dragged it into the room with the rest of me close behind.

"Where in the *hell* have you been?" the Sarge demanded. Her iron grip was cutting off the blood flow in my arm. The shrill cries continued. The Sarge shouted into my ear, "Your wife is in severe labor. You stay with her while I call her doctor."

"You've got it all wrong," I shouted back. "I'm not the husband. I'm the chaplain. I'm Joe!" I tapped my name tag. "Remember? We met? Just a few weeks ago."

Instructively, I pointed to the bellowing patient. "She needs a lot of help right now. I'm pretty sure none of it should come from me." My brain shifted into high gear. "Uh . . . uh," I stammered, nodding my head with conviction, "*Revelation* says so!"

With her free hand, the Sarge yanked on my tie, pulling my face down so we were nose to nose. I could smell coffee on her breath.

"Look, I don't care who you are," she said tightly. "And I sure as hell don't care what *Revelation* says, but you *will* stay with her. Do you hear me, *mister* chaplain?"

**Teachable moment number one:** *Do not discuss the* Book of Revelation *with a head nurse who is in the middle of a crisis.*

My theology now called for me to beg.

"Please, please, let me go," I cried. "What if, uh, what if something . . . you know, uh, happens? What if the . . . *something* happens? What do I do?"

"You're the chaplain aren't you?" the Sarge demanded. I nervously nodded. "Well then, dammit, son," she hollered. "*Pray!*" She let me go and left.

I approached the patient slowly. She was young and petite and looked like she had eaten a small cow. Slick strands of long, dark hair were plastered to her sweaty face. She was screaming wordlessly. I put my hands on the bed rail to steady myself.

"Sarge, she, ah . . . I mean your nurse, she told me . . . uh, I mean asked me, to stay with you while . . . while she gets your doctor. I'm the new chaplain, well, kind of new . . ." She sat up suddenly, clamped her fingers around my left hand and let loose with a string of obscenities. She squeezed so tightly she pressed my knuckles hard against my wedding ring, which caused me to join her in screaming, and we kept it up together until she let go.

**Teachable moment number two:** *It is a mistake to hold hands with a screaming woman in labor, especially if you are wearing a ring.*

Building trust and putting the patient at ease is the first principle a chaplain intern learns. To do just that, I sat in the chair next to her bed, lowered the bed rail, leaned forward a little to make good eye contact, and smiled reassuringly.

"So, tell me," I said casually. "When is your baby due?"

"What?" Her nostrils flared and eyes blazed. "When's my baby due?! Did you just ask me *when* my baby's due? *Right now, you moron! It's due right now!*"

**Teachable moment number three:** *Stupid questions do not build trust.*

"Please," I said. "I'm sorry. I've never done anything like this. I don't know what I'm supposed to say."

"Really?" she growled. "You had me fooled."

"Just tell me what to do, please."

"Hold my hand! Hold it, dammit," she shouted and wailed in pain, thrusting her open palm in my direction.

A delicate moment had arrived. I was determined not to say anything stupid.

That's when I said something stupid. Holding out my injured hand, I asked, "Do you think we could try something else? My hand *really* hurts."

When she spoke, her voice came out loud but in measured tones.

"Oh. So you hurt, do you? Here, let me help *you* feel *better*." In a flash, she grabbed my hand again and squeezed, much harder than before. As I hollered, another spasm hit her, and a spray of spit landed on my face, followed by screams and profanity.

**Teachable moment number four:** *Never tell a woman in labor that* you *hurt.*

After retrieving my aching hand once more, I desperately sifted through my alternatives. I spotted a wash cloth on the rack by the sink, rushed over, and wet it, then wiped off my face. The cool cloth was wonderful. Feeling better, I went back to her bedside. She leaned forward.

"Notice anything?" she said through clenched teeth.

"Ah . . . no. What? Well, I . . . I'm not sure. Tell me."

"My face, idiot, *my* face! Get *me* the damn wash cloth!"

This time, I leaned to one side when the spittle flew. I dashed to the sink, wet the wash cloth, rushed back, and applied it to her face and neck. She calmed enough to thank me.

Her spasms eased, and she calmed down even more. Only then did it occur to me that I didn't know her name.

"Mozelle," she told me wearily.

What kind of name was Mozelle, I wondered. Better not to ask.

"Named for my grandma," she said.

"My name's Joe, after my daddy. He's an obstetrician-gynecologist."

"Well, well," she snarled, her anger returning. "What the hell good does that do me?"

Another wave of pain rocked her, and she fumbled for my hand. I offered my good one, and she grabbed it, and we made a fist together. For the first time I saw fear in her eyes. I added my injured hand to the pile, and we sat in silence, our fist clenched as the pain came and went.

**Teachable moment number five:** *Silence trumps stupid questions.*

Pain-filled minutes crawled by with glacial slowness. Her labor spasms grew in frequency and strength. What the hell was taking the Sarge so long? For that matter, where was Mozelle's husband? This brought us back to stupid questions, but she was ahead of me.

"Don't be askin' me about Bubba," she hissed between clenched teeth, then used a string of expletives to describe Bubba's character and performance as a husband.

"His sorry no good ass was supposed to [*unprintable*] be here by now," she shouted. "He's probably out in the woods huntin'."

I winced at the name *Bubba*. Most guys and one girl with that name had beaten me up at one time or another, starting with a kid in kindergarten who bloodied my nose my first day at school. I thought fast.

"Ah . . . you don't, um . . . think Bubba's gonna, ah . . . mind me, um . . . being here with you, do you?"

"Who the hell *cares* what Bubba thinks? [*Unprintable*] him. Ain't nothin' ever bothers him less he's had a few beers."

Great. Just [*unprintable*] great. Bubba was gonna come in here and catch me holding hands with his Mozelle, and then he was gonna up and stomp me all over. Mozelle bolted straight up in bed and wailed like a banshee on a fire truck.

"Rub my back! Rub my back!" she screeched. "It hurts! *It hurts!* Rub it! Rub it!"

"What?" Now I was flustered. "*Me* rub *your* back? No. No no no, oh *hell* no!"

Great. Now I was cussing.

"Just hang on!" I cried. "The nurse is coming . . . I'm sure Bubba's gonna be here any minute. He'll rub your back!"

"*JUST DO IT,*" Mozelle shouted wild-eyed, spit flying everywhere. "I need it now! It hurts *now!*"

Years later, screaming women in labor would provide Nike with its now famous slogan.

Then, like the Sarge, Mozelle grabbed my tie and

jerked, pulling me close. I found myself within an inch of her enormous belly.

"Slide your hands under my back and start rubbing, you sonofa . . .! You *hear* me? *Rub. My. Back.*"

**Teachable moment number six is the big one:** *No matter what, chaplain interns should never ever visit a woman in labor. If you do, do not rub her back. If you do rub her back, do not do so in the following manner:*

Mozelle raised her hips, and I reached all the way over her swollen tummy and, off-balance, slowly slid my left hand under her right side and my right hand under her left side. A critical error. She immediately collapsed back onto the bed and almost pulled my shoulders from their sockets. My knees buckled. My cheek squished against her belly, causing my lips to pucker. I was trapped.

At this point I knew my life was over. At any moment Bubba, full of beer, would push his way through the door and find me gasping and all puckered up against his wife's belly. I felt his hands tightening around my neck. In muffled tones mixed with drool, I begged Mozelle to "Pweeze, pweeze, whet me go! Whet me go!" Frantically, I tried to wriggle my hands out from under her back. No such luck. I kept trying.

Then, inexplicably, Mozelle's screams ceased. Her silence was followed by deep guttural moans: "Oooh! Aaah! Right there! That's right! That's the spot! Ooh! Don't . . . stop! It feels sooo goood!" Wriggling my fingers under her back created a massaging effect. *Please, God, don't let Bubba come in.*

Light from the hall streamed in as the door swung opened. Mozelle moaned again. I turned my head just enough to draw breath and take a look. Sweat trickled down my brow. I wanted to see a pair of white nursing shoes squishing across the room. I took another glimpse. I drooled like a leaky faucet. There . . . a pair of dark muddy hunting boots coming toward me.

Bubba.

There was no way out. My fledgling career as a hospital chaplain was about to be cut short, all because of a woman in labor named Mozelle with a husband named Bubba.  At that moment, the Sarge's words popped into my mind. "You're a chaplain aren't you? Well then, dammit son, *pray!*"

With my head turned, I could speak and drool at the same time.

"Now ah way me down to sweep. I pray the Lhard ma soul to keep." From the corner of my eye I saw that Bubba had stopped and bowed his head. I kept praying, but now it came out, "Gawd is gwate. Gawd is good. Whet us tank him fowah owa foowahd."

Mozelle settled down. With one mighty final pull my sweaty hands slid free, and I hit the floor on my knees. There wasn't much time before Mozelle would be whooping and hollering again. Once more, the prayer changed, this time leaking out as The Lord's Prayer. It came out in fragments.

". . . but deliver us from evil . . . ." Dank mud odor filled my nose as I slunk past Bubba's boots. The door was near. ". . . for thine is the kingdom . . ." The Sarge and the doctor came in, and I passed them, and crossed the threshold. ". . . and the power . . ." The Sarge looked down at me and sneered.

"Coward," she spat. I didn't care. I had no dignity left.

The bright light of the hallway let me know I was finally free, that I had really reached the Promised Land, intact.

A loud screech split the air behind me. I smiled.

It was Bubba. He should have taken off that ring.

And so we come to **Teachable moment number seven:** *Often, the most powerful and authentic prayers are the spontaneous cries of the helpless.*

Despite all the technology and medicine available, it often comes down to the people in the room. Sometimes, all we can do is hold on to each other and scream and cuss and rage and recite nursery rhymes.

# 3

## *Snicker Snatch*

One Friday when I was seven, my mother greeted us in the kitchen with two candy bars, a Milky Way and a Snickers. Before Vicki could choose, I snatched the Milky Way, tore off the wrapper and devoured it. Vicki, who was nine, decided to save hers for later and put it high up in the kitchen cabinet.

After supper, Daddy was called to the hospital to deliver a baby. Vicki and I washed dishes while Mama put our baby brother Kenny to bed. At eight o'clock, we gathered before the warmed-up RCA television set ready for *Rawhide*, our show of shows. "*Rollin', Rollin', Rollin', Though the streams are swollen, keep them doggies rollin', Rawhide! Rain and wind and weather, Hell-bent for leather, Wishin' my gal was by my side.*" I didn't get all the words, but I liked the ones I got.

Every episode had a campfire scene. Rowdy, Mr. Favor, Wishbone and Mushy sat around the warm glow of flames. Suspended over the fire was a big black kettle that held the "grub." They chewed, smacked and swallowed with satisfaction, then sopped the gravy from their tin plates with bits of biscuits, gulped down coffee and wiped their mouths with the back of their hands.

All that chewing, smacking and swallowing reminded me that Vicki's candy bar was all alone in the kitchen cabinet. I wasn't really hungry, but I wanted some of that satisfaction and a Snickers had never let me down.

Rowdy's adventure unfolded on the screen, but all I saw was that candy bar going to waste up in the cabinet. When the first commercials came, I jumped up and mumbled something about the bathroom. My sister ignored me, and Mama told me not to wake Kenny. I didn't go to the bathroom. I went to the kitchen. With only a swinging door between me and Vicki and my mother, my mission called for stealth. I paced silently back and forth in front of the kitchen counter, waiting for the commercials to end. I would make my move when Rowdy had their attention. I had to act quickly.

I heard Mr. Favor's voice and swung up, cat-like, onto the counter. I opened the cabinet and eyed the top shelf. It was a bit of a reach, but on tiptoes, I groped around the shelf, careful not to disturb the spice tins or knock over the salt and pepper shakers. I knew it was there. It *had* to be there. I had seen her hide it. Time was short. Another commercial was coming. Then I found it, and my mouth watered. I took it from the shelf slowly. Delicious, chocolatey, nutty aromas tickled my nose. Paper crackled as I ripped off the wrapper. In three or four bites, I gobbled down my sister's scrumptious Snickers and licked my fingers.

I heard a commercial: *Brylcreem, Brylcreem, a little dab'll do ya!* I dropped lightly to the floor, tossed the crumpled wrapper in the trash can and slipped through the swinging door unnoticed. One commercial led to another, and I was warm and comfy with that candy bar inside me. The show returned, and I smiled at how well it had all worked out. My mother and Vicki only had eyes for the tall and handsome figure of a young Clint Eastwood, who was Rowdy Yates to me.

When the next batch of commercials came, Vicki got up and went into the kitchen. Maybe she was headed for the bathroom . . . but, no. I heard her clambering up on the kitchen counter. Her hand slapped around the cabinet shelf. Spice tins and salt and pepper shakers rattled. Then the kitchen door swung open, and Vicki loomed there in front of me, hands on hips. My throat tightened, and I gulped. I could still taste peanuts and chocolate.

"Where's my *Snickers* bar?" she demanded.

I glanced at the TV. Rowdy had the bad guy in his sights. He was ready to pull the trigger. The bad guy begged, "But, but, you, you've got it all wrong! It's all a misunderstanding!"

I began choking out my own series of "buts."

"But, but, but . . . wait a minute!" I cried. "I didn't do it! You don't know what you're talking about! I don't even *like* Snickers bars! They're too nutty."

"You took it." Vicki said it like it was a fact. Which it was. "You took it from the kitchen shelf and ate it."

"I did not!" I tried to think. "You're just mad because you lost it! Mama, tell her to quit picking on me!"

My mother was about to speak, but Vicki got there first.

"Mama, he did too eat it. It's in there!" My sister pointed at my stomach. And then she reared back and let me have it. The punch came out of nowhere and walloped me in the gut, and it *hurt*. She raised her fist to strike again, but Mama grabbed her arm.

I doubled over, not faking it but playing my pain for all it was worth.

"Mama, she hit me! Ooooh, my stomach hurts," I blubbered through not-completely feigned tears. "I didn't take her ol' candy bar! Make her stop!"

"Yes he did Mama! Look! There! Look at his mouth! Look!"

Still holding Vicki back, my mother leaned toward me, raised my chin and spotted a tiny smudge of chocolate in the corner of my mouth. A shot rang out from the TV. Rowdy Yates had gotten his man, and it was over for me, too. I knew that then. It's the little details that get you hung.

My mother released Vicki and used a fingernail to flick a crumb of peanut off my cheek.

"Let's go, young man!" She grabbed my arm so hard it hurt and marched me upstairs to face the music. Vicki laughed diabolically and threw a handful of *I told you so*'s up the stairwell.

In my bedroom, Mama delivered a swift series of stinging spanks.

"Please, Mama! Please! I'm sorry! I'll never do it again! Please! I didn't mean it!"

The spanking finally ended. At my mother's command, I got into my pajamas and crawled under the covers, sniffling for real. She sat on the edge of the bed.

"I'm so ashamed of you, Joe. You stole from Vicki and lied to me. Do you remember the story about Cain and

Abel?" My mother rarely went to church, but Bible stories at bedtime were common.

"The one where he kills his brother?" I wiped away my tears.

"That's the one."

"You mean Cain killed Abel because he wanted his candy bar? But I didn't do that! Vicki's the one who almost killed *me!*"

"Don't get smart with me, young man." I cringed. "Vicki didn't really hurt you. I'm not talking about killing. I'm talking about stealing and lying. You acted like Cain when you stole and lied. Cain stole his brother's *life* from him and then lied to God about it. You stole Vicki's candy and lied to her and me. Stealing is wrong. You made it worse when you lied about it."

"I didn't mean to lie."

"I know, but you did. That's why you got spanked. That's why I'm ashamed of you. You knew taking that candy was wrong, but you wanted it, and it got the better of you. You're young. These things happen. But when you were caught, the lie just slipped out without thinking, like it was an instinct."

"What's that?"

"Something you do without thinking. Like breathing."

"Breathing is good."

"But lying isn't, Joe. You have to learn what instincts to watch out for. Lying is one to stay away from. There are only two ways you can never get caught in a lie: you can teach yourself to be a really excellent liar, or you can not lie at all and not have to worry about it. How would you rather be known, as Joe the liar, Joe the thief? Or as Joe the straight shooter, the guy who tells the truth and leaves your stuff alone?"

"Tell the truth."

"That's right. You have to learn to set an example for Kenny. He's going to look up to his big brother someday."

"Yes, ma'am." That was a new thought for me.

"And think of this: how would things have gone if you had 'fessed up when Vicki found you out?"

"What do you mean?"

"What if you had up and admitted taking the Snickers? What would have happened?"

I thought for a minute. "I still woulda got a whipping."

"But not so hard, maybe." My mother nodded. "And it would have confused the heck out of Vicki."

She ruffled my hair and smiled.

"Do you remember the rest of the story?"

"No, ma'am, I don't."

"Well, Cain had to leave his home."

"I've got to *leave?*" My eyes grew wide.

"No, no. Cain had to leave his home because his sin was so big. We all have to pay for our sins. You were spanked and sent to bed and had to miss the rest of *Rawhide.*"

"Yes, ma'am."

"But there's more to the story, Joe. God let Cain start over. He put a mark on Cain's forehead to protect him, to remind him of what he'd done and warn him to not let his instincts get the better of him. Cain got a second chance to learn from his wrongs. You do too. This is it."

Mama ran her long red fingernails through my hair, then lightly kissed my forehead, leaving a smudge of red lipstick behind.

I woke the next morning to my mother's voice coming up from downstairs, calling Vicki and me to breakfast. I jumped out of bed and automatically made a beeline for the bathroom. Every morning Vicki and I raced to claim first dibs to the bathroom. This time, I beat her by a step.

I shut the door in her face and locked it. Vicki pounded the door, demanding that I let her in. I owed her, she shouted. Celebrating my victory, I backed away from the door pumping my fists into the air. That's when I caught myself in the mirror. The image startled me. There on my forehead were the remnants of red lipstick from my mother's kiss. I recalled her words about God's protective mark on Cain's forehead. A second chance.

I opened the door. Vicki was about to make another protest, but I stepped out of the bathroom and motioned her in. "I'm sorry I stole your Snickers," I said. "I won't do it again. I guess you can have mine next week."

She was speechless, and that felt good.

# 4

## *Resurrection at Applebee's*

After four counseling sessions it was lunchtime, and I was looking forward to an Applebee's Clubhouse Grill sandwich with fries and those little strips of dill pickle. I parked the car and got out, book in hand. A chilly October breeze greeted me that Tuesday as I made my way to the restaurant. I like my time alone, when I can have a quiet meal and read a book.

Halfway across the parking lot a man approached me. He could have been thirty or fifty. He looked like he'd been wearing the same clothes for a long while. Thick black bangs drooped down over his watery, red eyes.

"Mister, would you help me?" he asked. His Hispanic accent was thick. "I been putting roof on houses, you know, after the hail storm a few month ago. No work now. Please, if you could give me a few dollar for something to eat."

The few teeth he showed were chipped and decayed. He stood too close for comfort. When he spoke, a wave of bad breath punched me in the face. I could feel the stares of others hurrying by, glad they weren't me.

"No," I said resolutely. "No, I can't give you money." His head dropped, and he mumbled something in Spanish, perhaps a final plea. "No," I said, my voice louder. "Leave me alone." I turned and continued toward Applebee's. I'm not sure why, guilt I suppose, but after a few steps I stopped and looked back, hoping he was gone. There he stood.

"I won't give you money," I said, "but I will buy you a meal."

"Thank you, mister! Thank you much!" He hurried to catch up with me. When he did he patted me on the back with a rough, calloused hand. I bristled but tried not to show it.

We entered Applebee's, and the few minutes we waited seemed like forever. Finally the hostess arrived. "Two?" she said. "Smoking or non-smoking?" She thought I was with the Mexican.

"No, no," I said, embarrassed. "I'm not with him. I'm just paying for his meal." I breathed a sigh of relief as she led him to a stool at the bar. She came back and seated me in a booth. The young waitress who came to take my order had already been informed that I was paying for the Mexican's meal.

"Make sure he doesn't get any alcohol," I said. "And don't let him order more than ten dollars." She nodded and left.

Finally, alone and satisfied with my noble deed, I opened my book and began to read. But it was hard to concentrate. I kept glancing at the Mexican seated at the bar, his back to me. Three or four stools on either side separated him from the next person. Maybe I should have asked him to sit with me. I shook my head. The thought of it made me uncomfortable.

As the waitress brought my Clubhouse Grill, I saw his meal had also arrived. I bit into my sandwich and returned to my book, Thomas Cahill's *Desire of the Everlasting Hills: The World before and after Jesus*, which deals with the resurrection appearances. He refers to those privileged few, like Paul, who were eyewitnesses to such appearances. Cahill wonders about the rest of us, the ordinary folk, who never got a taste of the risen and exalted Jesus. Are we to be left only with faith?

Cahill found his answer in Matthew 25:35: "For I was hungry and you gave me food, I was thirsty and you gave me drink, I was a stranger and you took me in."

"Christians," Cahill wrote, "have never bothered to heed these solemn words about the presence of Christ in every individual who is in need."

I crunched down on a fry and thought, *Yeah! Cahill's got it. That's what resurrection means. We're all good at talking about it, we gladly attend sunrise services as long as breakfast is served afterwards, and we proudly place bumper stickers on our expensive cars proclaiming our readiness for the Rapture. But Jesus's resurrection appearances are meaningless if we don't reach out to the needy and the outcast. Jesus comes to us in the poor, the naked, the hungry, the ...* I stopped mid-thought.

There he sat at the bar. The Mexican. Ugly and disheveled with bad teeth and bad breath. There he was. Alone. A stranger. Probably an illegal alien.

Here I sat in my cushiony booth. A minister, a pastoral counselor. All right to look at. Maybe a little overweight. I floss and brush my teeth twice a day. My only crime is an occasional speeding ticket. Here I sat in my pale white skin, in my Polo shirt and pressed khakis.

I comforted myself. Everybody else had ignored him, but I had not. Talk about Matthew 25 – that's me!

Feeling better, I chomped down on a pickle and returned to Cahill. He tells of Dorothy Day, who founded the Catholic Worker movement in 1933. She spent her entire life in service to the hungry and the homeless. She said that without Christ's own words for it, it would seem "raving lunacy" to believe that any stranger is Christ. In her eyes, the goad of duty was unnecessary: "It is not a duty to help Christ, it is a privilege and not because these people remind us of Christ . . . but because they *are* Christ."

Her words stung. For me, it *was* the goad of duty. Everything inside me resisted helping that Mexican. I was embarrassed at the very idea of someone thinking I was associated with him. I felt no privilege here. *He* should feel privileged. He was lucky to find a sucker who would at least buy him a meal. I had even walked into the restaurant with him.

I glanced at him again still hunched over his plate, wolfing his meal. More guilt came. How easy it is to say we believe in the resurrection, but how hard it is to "do" gospel – to get close to and mingle with the poor, the hungry and the outcast.

Lost in thought, I didn't notice when the waitress came back to my table.

"He didn't buy any liquor," she said and placed the bill face down on the table. I glanced over at the bar again, but he was gone. My eyes shot to the door. Was that him leaving? I couldn't tell.

Cahill concludes, "The Good Samaritans of this world . . . see only the man fallen among thieves, the person who needs help. They do not see Christ."

I closed the book with a sigh and checked the bill. His part came to $8.95. I laid it down on the table and then just as quickly picked it back up.

Had my eyes tricked me? On the ticket was a note – not one of those cutesy waitress notes, but a message from him. I read it, then read it again.

"Thank you, Mister," it read. "I never know your name. The meal it was real good. You a good guy. God bless you."

He signed it. Signed it in the most common of all Mexican names: Jesus. He had come to me as a poor, filthy, foul-breathed Mexican. And I had not recognized him. We could have shared a meal, but I wouldn't let him sit at my table. I had shouted at him. I had told him to leave me alone. And I was glad it only cost me $8.95.

I had seen the Christ but had missed the privilege.

# 5

## *Alligator Belt*

"Do you have any threes?" I asked, knowing she did. We were sitting on the grass in her backyard. Reluctantly, she handed them over. Then, with a wide grin, I laid down my cards and looked at her. I had won the game of "Go Fish." Now for my prize.

I waited. I was looking forward to seeing an older woman (she was ten) take off her clothes.

Instead, Shelley jumped up and ran.

*This wasn't fair! I'd won! She owed me!* I ran after her. I caught her in my backyard. We wrestled a bit until I jerked down her Bermuda shorts exposing her backside. She began making a noise, something between crying and screaming, and she clung to a tree.

"Joe Baroody, what's going on?" Mama was standing at the backdoor. Shelley quickly pulled up her shorts and ran home, still crying. "Get in this house!" Mama shouted. As I walked through the door she spoke the words of doom: "Just wait 'til your father gets home!"

I knew what that meant. I would soon face the dreaded alligator belt.

One agonizing hour later, the tires of my dad's car crunched the gravel in the driveway. Crunched. That about summed it up. My mother briefed him on the events of the afternoon. When I heard him call my name, I knew what I was in for.

Daddy had a procedure for everything, including spanking. I knew to stand perfectly still and silent while he carefully sifted through the belts hanging in his closet. I saw that he selected the alligator belt, held it up for inspection, folded it in half and snapped it. I jumped at the sound of the loud pop. At his gesture I bent over the bed, gritted my teeth and waited.

And waited.

Always methodical, Daddy aligned my hips, smoothed the wrinkles on my jeans, lightly patted my rear and said, "You ready?" *What a question! Did it really matter? Just get on with it!* Slowly the seconds ticked away. Like Arnold Palmer at the golf tee, Daddy gave a few practice swings. I felt the belt brush against me. More seconds passed. The Day of the Lord had arrived. I braced myself for the blow. It came swift and sure, but it was not the one I expected.

His hand gently squeezed the back of my neck. "Sit up here, Junior Joe Boy."

Daddy patted the bed. "We need to talk about what you did." He lay the belt aside. *Oh, no. A talk. I didn't want to talk. I preferred the sting of the alligator belt over a talk. Anything but that.*

Daddy began: "Your granddaddy Papa Joe once caught me stealing a stick of peppermint candy. I was about eight or so, around your age. He spanked me with this belt." Daddy held up the alligator belt. "Scared the daylights out of me. You know what I learned?"

I shook my head.

"I learned not to get caught."

He was silent. "How would you like it if someone pulled your pants down?" Daddy quizzed. Tears came to my eyes. Daddy paused. He lifted my chin and looked intently at me.

"Someone did," I blubbered. I told him about the time some older guys had carried me into an old shack after a game of baseball. They pulled off my clothes, threw them onto the field and ran away laughing.

"How did that make you feel?" Daddy asked.

"Not good," I said.

"How do you think Shelley felt today?"

Daddy pulled me against his chest. I didn't really remember much more of the talk, just the warmth of his hug and some Bible verse about mercy and justice.

Justice – the lesson of right and wrong – was not rendered by the alligator belt that day. Rather it came from my dad's words of mercy, the empathy I felt for Shelley and the humility I felt in his hug.

# 6

## *Selling Apples on Saturday*

After a particularly intense week as a hospital chaplain, I was emotionally drained, ready to shift gears, let go, relax. I was looking forward to a weekend off and thought I might be able to leave the hospital early. I wanted to go home, kiss my wife, hug my kids, sit in front of the television, eat supper and watch Vanna White turn those letters on *Wheel of Fortune*. I loved Vanna. Told my wife I wanted to marry her. That was okay with Nancy. She planned to marry Tom Selleck from *Magnum, P.I.*

My beeper went off before I could leave, calling me to the intensive care unit. A seventy-two year-old farmer had just died of heart failure. I did not know this man. I had never visited him or met his two daughters, who waited in the family room and wanted a chaplain to go with them to see their father's body. I headed to the unit, hoping I could take care of the matter with dispatch.

The women were tearful but not distraught. Their father had suffered for months, and he was finally at peace. All the better, I told myself. A peaceful, expected death made my job straightforward. Go with them to the room, say a prayer, offer consolation and comfort, gather the deceased's belongings and make sure the funeral home was notified. Piece of cake. I'd have them in and out of there in no time.

Fifteen minutes later we were in the lobby, and I was patiently ushering the daughters to the exit when two little girls dashed through the door and ran to their mother. Their neighbor had brought the girls just in time. Their mother introduced me to the neighbor and then to the girls, who were Amy, four, and Tammy, five. They had big blue eyes and shoulder-length blonde hair. They might have been twins. I greeted them with a pat on the head and resumed my efforts to move the family, and me, out the door.

I felt a tug on my pants leg.

"Will you take us to see Granddaddy?" Amy said. "We want to see him."

Tammy nodded solemnly. "Mommy said we could see Granddaddy."

I took their mother aside. Did they know he had died? They did. She had phoned from the family room and told the girls the news. They begged to come, she said, to see him one last time. She had agreed, hoping they would change their minds once they got to the hospital. Normally children their age aren't allowed in the intensive care units, and I told her the final decision was up to the nurses.

They waited outside while I checked.

"You know they're too young," one nurse said. Another lamented being forced to view her uncle in his casket.

"I was seven," she said. "Ruined me for life."

Under my breath I muttered, "That didn't do it," and wondered where that bit of bitterness had come from. Becky, the dead man's nurse that day, said it should be okay, but to be sure she called his doctor, who kicked the decision right back to her.

"Let's take them in," she said. "I'll go with you."

"You okay?" she said as we left the unit. "You were muttering."

"Sorry." I blushed. "I'm a little tired. Been a long week. These kids messed up my plans. I'd hoped to leave early, get home in time for *Wheel of Fortune*."

"Still planning to marry Vanna?"

"Yep."

Becky took the girls aside while I spoke to their mother, who had decided to wait in the hall with her sister and the neighbor.

"Are you sure about this?" My voice had more edge in it than I intended.

"They'll be all right. We talked about this, and they want to do it on their own. They'll be fine." She looked at her daughters, who were looking at her.

"Go ahead, girls," she said. Without hesitation, Amy took my hand, and Tammy reached for Becky's.

The room was cluttered with inert medical machines. A cardiac monitor mounted on the wall was dark, the ventilator beside it silent. An IV pole, pushed out of the way, held partially full bags of fluid. A soft brown hospital blanket covered the body up to the neck. His eyes and mouth were closed, his thin, gray hair neatly combed. The weather-beaten face spoke of decades of hard work in the sun. The features were peaceful now, at rest.

As soon as we were in the room, Amy and Tammy dropped our hands and went to the bedside. We waited in the doorway.

"Wow," Tammy said. "This is the big bed Mommy told us about. I thought it was gonna be bigger."

Amy touched the ventilator. "This helped Granddaddy breathe."

Tammy pointed to the IV pole. "That stuff that made him feel better."

At the foot of the bed the girls slid their hands over the soft bedspread. Amy bumped his foot and looked back to us apologetically, tears trembling in her eyes. Her sadness touched me. I started toward them, but Becky stopped me.

"Wait," she whispered. "They're all right."

Tears rolled down their cheeks. Their small hands moved gently along the blanket, making their way slowly to the head of the bed. After a moment of looking at him and fussing with his pillow, Amy pulled a footstool over to the bed and stood on it. She looked at her grandfather's leathery face, touched his cheek and petted his stiff, snowy whiskers. She turned and helped her sister onto the stool, and Tammy patted his chest and sniffled. After a long moment, Amy took her sister by the arm and helped her off the stool. They hugged for a moment, then locked hands and rushed past us and out of the room.

It took only a few minutes, but that's an eternity when you're holding your breath. I drew in air raggedly, and Becky did the same.

Outside, the girls clung to their mother, sobbing. The mother saw me and gave me an imploring look. I nodded and went over, getting down on one knee so I could see the girls. "I'm sorry about your grandfather," I said. I wasn't very good at talking with kids. They looked at me expectantly, both of them sniffling.

"What was that like for you?" I asked, hoping they might want to talk about what had just happened. I don't know what I expected, but Amy's answer caught me off guard.

"On Saturdays he took us to sell apples," she said. "It was fun. He gave us candy and let us sit in the back of his truck with all the baskets of apples. He had a chair next to the truck, and he talked to people. Everybody knew Granddaddy." She paused, and I could see her expression change.

"Granddaddy won't take us to sell apples anymore, will he," she said.

Tammy rubbed her eyes with her fists, then looked at me.

"Granddaddy's gone to heaven, hasn't he? Mommy says old people get sick, and then they go to heaven." She hesitated, glanced at her sister. "He won't come see us anymore, will he? That's right, isn't it?"

"That's right." My voice cracked. "Granddaddy is in heaven."

They knew it all already.

"Girls, we'd better get going." Their mother nudged them, her own tears falling onto the front of her blouse.

They turned to go, but Amy came back and took my hand in hers and put her mouth next to my ear.

"Thanks for taking us to see Granddaddy," she whispered. She turned and ran and caught up with her mother and sister as they stepped onto the elevator. The doors had almost closed when Amy suddenly dashed out, and her mother's hand caught the door.

"I forgot," she said cheerfully as she slid to a stop. "I've got something for you."

She dug into her pocket and pulled out a worn, bent stick of Juicy Fruit gum. Its rumpled yellow wrapper said it had been in her pocket a while.

"You look sad," she said. "When we got sad Granddaddy gave us some gum and hugged us around our necks." She shoved the gum into my hand and threw her arms around my neck and squeezed. And then she was gone.

"Thank you," I whispered to elevator doors.

Still on my knees, I looked at her gift and felt the weight of the week lifting.

Amy did for me what I could not do for myself. She gave comfort to the comforter.

I stood up, peeled off the battered wrapper, pushed the gum into my mouth and chewed. I savored the sweetness as I walked outside.

# 7

## *Proper Pedaling Procedure*

"We line up single file," Daddy said. "I lead. Joe-Joe . . . *Junior Joe Boy!*" He thumped my ear. "You listening?" He always called me Junior Joe Boy when he wanted to make sure I heard him.

"Yessir." I nodded. Vicki elbowed me in the side. She took great pleasure in my mishaps.

"As I was saying. Joe, you line up behind me. Sister Vick, you bring up the rear."

"Yes, sir," my big sister said.

It was a pleasant September Sunday afternoon. We were about to embark on a bike ride, something we'd never done with Daddy. Thus, he subjected us to his lecture on the rules for having a "safe and pleasurable biking experience." This talk, which I call "Proper Pedaling Procedure," became another excerpt from his unwritten "Proper Preparation Procedures Avoid Pointless Problems" manual. Besides having a procedure for everything, Daddy liked alliteration.

Vicki was actually being patient, but I had ants in my pants. My parents' birthday gift to me leaned on its kickstand right outside the back door – a shiny new metallic red Schwinn Cruiser with a two-tone leather seat. I was ready to fly.

"Next," Daddy said, "stick together, stay on the side

of the road in single file." Daddy's eyes bore down on me. "Nothing fancy. Maintain, I repeat, maintain a straight line at all times.

"Now, let's go over proper hand signals." Daddy turned his back to us. *Dear God, here it comes. The Demonstration.* "This is the correct signal for making a right turn."

He extended his left arm straight out, then bent it at the elbow into a perfect right angle, bending and extending his finger.

"Notice the index finger. It's a little something extra I've added. It's like a car's turn signal with the blinker flashing on and off." To demonstrate a left turn, Daddy straightened out his arm, and, pointing to the left, "blinked" his index finger.

He turned back to face us. "Now let me see both of you do it." Three times we repeated the turns, using our index finger to blink. I was sure he'd lost his mind.

"Finally, a word about speed," my father said, looking at me. Vicki was twelve and responsible. I was ten and not. "And that word is *slow*. We are in no hurry, right Junior Joe Boy?"

"Yessir."

"Okay then," he rubbed his hands together. "Head 'em up. Move 'em out!"

Outside, my bike gleamed in the September sun. I inspected it with a critical eye and liked what I saw. I brushed off the seat, shook the big chrome basket attached to the front, and tested the feel and sturdiness of the handlebars. I crouched down to study the chain and chain guard, and both looked good.

I checked the spokes to make sure all the baseball cards were secure. With enough speed, their buzzing sounded like a racecar engine. Mickey Mantle, Roger Maris and Willie Mays looked up at me, ready to go. I stroked the shiny red crossbar with its snazzy white stripes. I looked at my father and sister sitting on their bikes, waiting for me at the end of the driveway. Speed, not slow, was the word. That was my plan.

In one swift motion my right foot snapped back the kickstand, my hands gripped the handlebars, and I swung my leg over the seat, mounting the bike like Roy Rogers mounted Trigger – a movement that required careful calculation to avoid a painful landing. I had already practiced this move a few dozen times since breakfast. I kicked off and hit the pedals, pumping up some speed before I slammed on the brakes and skidded to a stop between my father and sister, gravel flying. Vicki rolled her eyes. Daddy gave me one of his piercing remember-what-I-told-you stares.

Looking both ways, Daddy signaled a right turn. Vicki and I followed close behind, our index fingers blinking. We were moving so slowly it was hard to steer straight. We trundled along, stopping for cars to pass. If my father turned left at the intersection ahead, we would circle out onto a busy road. For my plan to work, we needed to go straight across.

After stopping to check traffic, he led us straight ahead. Great! My plan was unfolding nicely. Next to us on the left was a wide grassy median divided by a ditch. This led up to the focus of my attention – a ramp my buddies and I had built out of a slab of plywood and three wooden boxes. Starting at the edge of the median, we would build speed, hit the ramp and, if all went well, sail over a three-foot-wide ditch.

We neared the ramp, and I tightened my grip on the handlebars, lifted up from my seat and leaned forward, narrowing my eyes. I cut to my left and pedaled for glory. The baseball card motor hummed. The wind made it hard to see and blew my brushcut back. I flew across the median, ramp in my sights. Behind me, faint under the hum of the baseball cards, I heard my father and sister yelling. It sounded like they were cheering me on.

I approached the ramp at full bore, aiming for the middle for a solid lift-off. I shot a glance over my shoulder. Vicki waved and yelled, but I didn't see my father. I glanced back again, which turned out to be the wrong place to put my attention. I hit the ramp off center and slid off the plywood, plunging into the ditch. My feet left the pedals and I somersaulted over the handlebars and flew as if in slow motion, landing on my back.

A couple of kids on bikes had stopped to watch me fly. Vicki left her bike and sprinted toward me. The impact of the landing knocked the breath out of me. My sister cleared the ditch in a leap and knelt beside me.

The guys on the bikes, my friends who had often jumped the ditch with me, were laughing.

"Look at Baroody," they hooted. "He busted his butt!"

"You okay?" Vicki helped me up. I bent over, hands on my knees. I nodded.

"Daddy's hurt," she said. "When he shouted at you to stop, he fell off his bike and cut his hand."

We walked together toward my father. He was sitting on the side of the road, holding his bloody hand. His bike was several feet away.

"Are you all right?" He grimaced.

"Yes, sir, I'm . . . okay." I stared at his dripping hand.

"Get your bike and go home. Now. Vicki will see you get there. I'll be home in a little bit."

Vicki helped me drag my bike from the ditch. The front wheel was warped and bent. Spokes poked out every which way, baseball cards scattered everywhere. "What in the world were you thinking?"

"How bad is Daddy's hand?' I asked. "Is he gonna be all right?"

"He'll be fine," she said, but I didn't believe her. "Let's just get home. He told us to get home. I can't believe you did that!"

My new bright, shiny bike was too busted to push. I started crying, threw it down, and took off running. Thoughts raced through my mind. What if Daddy couldn't be a doctor anymore? What if he couldn't deliver babies? It was my fault. What had I been thinking? My sister called to me to wait, but I kept running and crying.

I rushed through the front door. My mother was resting on the sofa. She sat up as I ran through the room.

"Joe, what's wrong?" she called. "Where are Daddy and Vicki?" I ran past her to my bedroom and crawled into my closet. I shut the door and curled up in the dark on top of my toy box.

I heard Vicki telling Mama what happened. The front screen door slammed shut again. There was more excited chatter, this time between my parents. Then I heard the sound of water running in the kitchen sink and cabinet doors clicking shut.

The belt would be welcome. I more than deserved it. My bedroom door opened, and my father's footsteps crossed the room. My closet door opened, and a bandaged hand pushed apart the hanging clothes. I was ready to be called out to face my punishment.

But Daddy didn't order me out. Instead, he squeezed in the closet and shut the door behind him. I sobbed, breathing in the smell of antiseptic.

"My hand is fine, son," he said. "Just a shallow cut. It looked worse than it was."

I raised my head, and he showed me his bandaged hand, using it as a puppet while explaining proper bandaging procedure. I laughed a little.

Pushing more clothes to the side, Daddy reached into his pocket and brought out a rock. I recognized it as one of the larger rocks from the driveway. I was confused.

"I think we can agree you did a reckless thing," he said.

"Yes, sir. We can."

"And that you broke the rules."

"Yes, sir." Tears welled up in my eyes again. "But I wanted to impress you. I wanted you to be proud of what I could do."

He reached for me and I cringed, but he hugged me close and tousled my hair and kissed me where the cowlick grew.

"I know, son," he said in a whisper. "And I am."

"You are?" My voice trembled.

"Well, not today so much, but generally."

It took a moment for me to get my head around that.

"You mean I don't get the belt?"

"Not this time. This time you get a little amnesty."

"What's that?"

"No belt."

"No belt? How come?"

"I'm guilty, too." He turned the rock around in his hand. "When I was your age, I got into several scrapes trying to impress your grandfather. He was a hard man to impress. I suppose maybe I am, too."

"No, Daddy, I . . ." I was crying again. "I was just showing off."

"I know, son. It's the same thing."

"It is?"

He nodded.

"So . . . no belt?" I asked.

"Do you want the belt?"

"No, sir. I do not."

"I can't give you the belt because I'm guilty of the same sin." He shrugged. "I can't cast the first stone."

I must've shown my confusion.

"You remember the story about Jesus and the woman? The woman caught in adultery."

"I remember she was gonna get stoned to death for something, right?"

"Yes. Do you remember why?"

"No, sir."

"Well, it was a big crime. The punishment for adultery was death by stoning. Jesus said it was all right with him if they stoned her, but he insisted that only someone who had never done anything wrong could be allowed to throw the first stone. None of the religious leaders could say they had never done anything wrong."

I thought for a moment.

"Everybody sins, right?"

"That was his whole point." He nodded and smiled. "And the woman had paid a price for her crime – she was caught in the act, and she was embarrassed and ashamed. And you get off with this little talk for the same reason. Because on this matter, I can't judge you, and I won't. I saw those guys riding by and laughing at you. I imagine you had bragged to them about how good you were at jumping that ditch."

I looked down.

"You also wanted to show me what you could do with your new bike. But you crashed the bike, and then you felt shame and guilt because of that, and because I fell off my bike and cut my hand."

"I was scared you couldn't be a doctor anymore."

"And I was scared you'd broken your neck." He grinned. "We were both wrong. But sometimes the consequences of our behavior are punishment enough."

I breathed a sigh of relief.

"So, Junior Joe Boy, you're being let off the hook," he said. "But you get the same warning as the woman in the Bible: go and sin no more."

"Watch my step," I said. "Don't break the rules."

"Don't break the rules," my father agreed.

He brushed my cheek with the back of his good hand. As we clambered out of the closet, I said, "You know, I really *can* jump that ditch. I hold the record ..."

My father shook his head. "You can't jump the ditch if you don't have a bike. Yours is still back there with a broken front wheel. And your old one is mine. Remember, sometimes the consequences of our behavior carry their own punishment."

"Oh. Right." I had to risk one more question. "Since you're not going to stone me, why do you have that rock?"

"You keep it." He tossed it to me. "A reminder of our talk."

I turned the rock over in my hand. Painted on it in blue was this: "John 8:7. *He that is without sin among you, let him first cast a stone at her.*"

Today that rock sits on my office desk – the same desk that once occupied my daddy's office. It reminds me to be careful how I respond to those who sit in front of me, confessing their wrongs – that I, too, am guilty of sin.

# 8

## *Talking to the Dead*

"What are you doin' up, butthead?" I said when my brother poked his face into the den.

"Shh." He held a finger to his lips.

"You're supposed to be in bed."

"I know, I know," Kenny whispered. "Don't get bent out of shape. We have to talk, Joe. It's important." He looked desperate, not that I cared.

"Don't bother me. *Bonanza*'s on." I was a senior in high school and had the privilege of staying up past ten o'clock. On this Sunday night, everyone else had gone to bed early, and I had the television to myself. During one of the commercial breaks, I had picked up the Bible, the "King Jimmy," as Daddy liked to call it. When Kenny entered the room, I snapped it shut and stashed it behind the couch cushion.

"It can't wait, Joe," Kenny insisted. "It's about Mama. I'm worried about her. We've got to do something. You know she smokes too much. If we don't do something, she's gonna die."

"You're an idiot. Mama's too ornery to die. Besides, the dead people don't want her. She bothers them too much already."

Mama liked talking to dead people. She often invited psychics to our home to give each family member a "reading," even Daddy.

I knew Kenny was thinking about Grandpa Kin, Mama's father. He had died four years earlier at sixty-three from lung cancer, compliments of his two-pack-a-day habit. Kin was by far Mama's favorite dead person to talk to. Kenny's fear for our mother had set his mind to work, and he devised a plan to get her to quit smoking. This is what he snuck into the den to tell me. I didn't protest when he clicked off the television.

"Okay. Here's what we do," he said, glancing over his shoulder. "We take some of her cigarettes. We cut them in half. We put them on the kitchen counter, making them spell K-I-N. In the morning she comes in and sees his name written in cut cigarettes. She'll think he sent her a message to quit smoking." He looked closely at me. "It could work. It could get her thinking. Come on."

"She'll just tell us to go get the board."

"Yeah, but she'll *believe*, Joe. You know she will. It'll work. Let's go."

"You really are a butthead. We're not doing anything. You're going back to bed," I said with authority as I followed him into the kitchen.

Kenny took five Pall Malls from the red pack next to the ashtray on the kitchen counter. With scissors from the drawer, he proceeded to cut each one in half. He handed them to me, and I arranged them on the kitchen counter to spell out KIN.

As Kenny reached to put back the scissors, he accidently knocked over Mama's casserole-sized ashtray. It landed on the floor with a loud crash, shattering, butts and ashes everywhere. Kenny and I looked at each other with instant horror and made a swift and silent beeline for bed as a door opened and Mama's slippers scudded into the hallway, headed for the kitchen.

Her scream pierced the night. "In here! Albert! Albert! Get in here!"

My dad's feet hit the floorboards and thumped toward the kitchen. Kenny and I looked at each other. We had to "get up" too. I tore off my clothes and threw on my pajamas.

In the kitchen we found Mama in her robe with her hair in curlers. One hand covered her mouth, and the other pointed back and forth from the broken ashtray on the floor to the carefully arranged cigarettes on the table. She was carrying on about a message from Kin. My father, in his boxer shorts, tried to soothe her.

"Now, now, Hazel," he said calmly. "We don't know what this is, what it means." He turned to us with a pointed look. "Do we, boys? Do we know what this is?"

Our faces registered the requisite surprise and indignation, and we slipped right into our denial.

"I went to bed right after *Bonanza*," I lied.

"I went to bed when y'all did," Kenny chimed in on cue.

"You're . . . *sure*?" My father appraised us critically and carefully, using his patented I-see-right-through-you look. We nodded in unison. He looked at us a moment longer, then turned back to Mama.

"Well," he said. "*Something* happened here." He patted her shoulder. "I doubt that someone broke into the house, but I'll check around." He looked at us again and spoke carefully to Mama. "Call the police, please. Keep the boys here."

My heart hit the floor. The *police*. Not the police! Still in his boxers, my father got his double-barrel shotgun and began checking the doors and windows. Mama dialed. Kenny and I stood there, frozen. Police *never* came to our house, especially on a Sunday night. And my daddy never ran around the house in his underwear, shotgun or no shotgun. Some minutes later, flashing red and blue lights lit up our driveway. My father found his bathrobe and put the gun away. Through the front window, I saw two uniformed officers get out and approach the house. One was a young patrolman; the other was older and wore sergeant's stripes.

Daddy answered the door, warmly greeting the sergeant. They knew each other from church. My father ushered them inside and told them briefly what happened. He showed them the halved cigarettes, the broken ashtray and the mess on the floor. He said he'd checked all the doors and windows and found no sign of a break-in. The sergeant studied the mess, glanced around the kitchen and eventually his gaze fell on Kenny and me. I don't think we were actually sweating, but it felt like it. Our hearts were pounding so loud we almost missed it when he told the patrolman to take my mother and father around the house, just to make sure things were okay.

"I'll have a little chat with the boys," he said.

My father sent us into the den but first gave us his no-nonsense look.

"You tell the *truth*, now," Dad said tightly. As we left he leaned close to the sergeant, and they whispered back and forth. The sergeant nodded and my father nodded back.

Swallowing hard, Kenny and I led the way to the den and took our seats on the sofa. The sergeant stood before us, hands on hips. He looked down at us and shook his head.

Several times he stopped himself just before he started to speak. He looked back to the empty doorway, put his hands in his pockets, and rocked back and forth on the balls of his feet, studying us each in turn. He was in no hurry.

I was ready, and I knew Kenny was, too. We had been here before. We were salted. Not with the police, maybe, but this wasn't our first interrogation. He was going to ask if we knew anything, if we had heard anything. He was going to ask if this was just a prank and we were too afraid to tell our parents. We were prepared and ready to look him right in the eye and lie.

But looking the sergeant in the eye was not simple – not because he was intimidating, though he was, but mostly on account of his lazy right eye, which stared at something behind us while the left eye bore down on us. It was disconcerting. You didn't know which eye to lie to.

We were getting jittery. I could feel Kenny about to explode. Just when I thought he couldn't stand it anymore, the sergeant crouched down in front of us.

"Did you mean to break the ashtray?" he asked.

"No," I heard myself say as Kenny said the same.

"It was an accident," I said.

"It was my idea," Kenny added quickly.

"Okay, then." The sergeant smiled and nodded. He patted us both on the back. "I think we're done here." He stood and turned and left the den. Kenny and I exchanged confused looks. After a moment, we got up and headed into the kitchen.

Daddy and the sergeant whispered to each other. They glanced at us, back at each other, and then nodded as if something had been decided. The sergeant put out a hand, and my father shook it. They slapped each other on the back, and the sergeant and the patrolman left through the front door, each assuring my mother that everything was fine. My father shut the door behind them. With his back to Mama, he gave Kenny and me a brief grin and a half-wink.

The front door had barely closed when Mama spoke up.

"Get the board, Kenny!" she called and went to the kitchen to clear the table. "I know it's Kin! I just know it! He's got something to say."

*Uh oh. Time to talk to the dead again.*

While other kids' mothers had bridge clubs, my mother had a weekly automatic writing group, country club women waiting for a spirit to possess them and scrawl out words of wisdom. I had passed through the kitchen many times while the possessed scrawled. One handed me a note from a spirit named "Julius" who came from the beyond to say "Hi" to me, and to claim we had served together as Roman legionnaires. Julius also said that, in my Roman days, Mama had been my sister.

My mother had tried repeatedly to contact her father.

She knew he had a message for her from the other side, something important, and she was determined to have it.

Kenny returned with the Ouija board and sat down at the kitchen table with Mama. The board worked best when it was just them. Daddy and I stood apart to watch. Mama took a deep breath and slowly exhaled, then did it again and then again. In a meditative voice, she began the ritual.

"Are there spirits among us?" After a moment the planchette slowly moved to the *Yes* and then veered away.

"Is there a spirit who wishes to speak?" *Yes.*

"What is this spirit's name?" The planchette haltingly spelled *K* then *I* then *N*.

My mother gave my father an I-told-you-so look. Kenny shot me a sly smile. For more than an hour Mama questioned Kin, her father, while Ken, her son, supplied the answers.

Like it or not, this was a regular family scene, our flavor of quality time. We were all gathered around the kitchen table, three generations of us if you count Kin, doing what families do – talk to each other. Did it matter that it was all based on a lie? Did it matter that it was the middle of the night, and the police had just left? Did it matter that my father, a distinguished man of medicine and faith, had scurried around the house clad in his boxer shorts and armed with a shotgun? Did it matter that Kin had been dead four years and the only person who believed he was actually in the room was my mother? Not if Mama quit smoking, it didn't. And she did – for three interminable and agonizingly hellacious months. On the day I rear-ended a pickup truck with her car, she lit one up.

In the end, Kenny's fear that Mama would die from cigarette smoking was accurate. Twenty-five years later, Mama succumbed to emphysema. Daddy died of lung cancer a few months earlier, likely from secondhand smoke.

Families are erratic and messy. But it is sometimes in the brokenness that we find our blessings. Even families like mine, huddling together after midnight, talking to the dead.

# 9

## *The Smithfield Girls*

My cousin Stewart and I had just returned from an afternoon of water-skiing. We were at the family dinner table at the lake house. It was Labor Day weekend.

"Stewart and I have dates tonight," I mentioned casually. The table went silent. I explained we had met two young ladies out on the lake. And, being experienced men of the world, we convinced them that a night out with us would be time well spent. I did not mention the terrifically tiny bikinis they wore.

Stewart grinned. Vicki snorted. Kenny wanted to know just who these lucky girls were.

"They're Ann and Jenna Smithfield, Jim Smithfield's daughters." Mr. Smithfield owned the station where we gassed up the boat. At the mention of their names, Daddy had a coughing spell. Apparently some iced tea had gone down the wrong pipe. Stewart and I retreated to our room to get ready for our evening out. On the way, I stopped by Daddy's dresser to borrow his bottle of English Leather.

I was in the bathroom squishing pimples when I heard Mama burst into the bedroom, shouting, "Stewart Haskin! You and Joe are *not* going out with *those* girls!" I figured since I was in the bathroom, I was, at least for the moment, in the clear. So I turned on the shower and took off my cut-offs. Mama threw open the bathroom door. I fell into the shower, scrambling to get back into my shorts.

"Get out here right now!" she shouted. Daddy, Vicki and Kenny had already gathered in the hallway. Stewart, still in his underwear, tried to cover himself up with his hands while Mama wagged her index finger in my face.

"Those girls are *sluts!* You and Stewart are *not* going out with them!"

I could not believe Mama called them sluts.

"They are not sluts!" I said. "What makes you think they are sluts?"

Mama carried on about the flimsy halter-tops their mother wore and how she eyed every man who pulled in for gas and how she had even "sidled" over to Daddy one day to ask if he needed help filling up the boat.

I was ready to jump in, but Stewart gained the courage to speak.

"Well, you know," he said, "they did seem kind of sluttish."

*Great, Stewart. Big help.*

"Look, Mama, I don't care what you say. They *aren't* sluts and we *are* going out with them."

"If you do, you will be sorry," Mama promised and grabbed for my arm. Daddy stepped in, pulled Mama away and led her out of the room. Just before they cleared the doorway, Daddy turned his head and said over his shoulder, "Don't stay out too late, boys."

The four of us decided on a little night club just across from Shaw Air Force Base. Stewart and Ann led the way through the noisy, smoky darkness. On our right was the bar, three-deep with thirsty customers. Before us were tables, with a dance floor beyond where a crowd of couples were shagging to the Tams' "I Been Hurt." Before the Austin Powers movies, the term *"shag"* refers to The Shag, a spirited swing-dance from 1959, inspired by the Lindy Hop and the Jitterbug, and the official South Carolina state dance since 1990.

We found a table, got settled and a waitress came. The sisters ordered Cokes and Stewart and I followed suit. From the speakers blared the Platters' "Up On The Roof."

"Wanna dance?" Stewart asked Ann.

"Yes, please," she said. They jumped up and dashed for the dance floor.

Stewart's wiry legs made shagging look easy. He and Ann moved like they knew what the other would do next. *How did they do that?* I had no grasp of the intricate niceties of the dance, so I made small talk with Jenna. I was pretty awkward at that, but she didn't seem to mind. I could tell she really wanted to dance.

My dancing talents were best displayed with up-tempo music. I could twist my hips and jerk my arms and legs while maintaining an ultra-cool grimace on my face. These spastic gyrations and the basic ballroom box-step pretty much rounded out my dancing repertoire.

Otis Redding started singing "Sittin' on the Dock of the Bay." I took that as my cue to dazzle Jenna with my ballroom moves. We assumed the classic dance position with just enough distance, as the Catholics say, for the Holy Ghost to fit between us.

"I Got the Fever," by Billy Scott and the Georgia Prophets, was next. It was as fast a song as I could hope for and gave me the window I needed to display my real talent. I was ready. I was on. I let myself *go!* I spun and twisted, then jerked my arms like they were crawling with fire ants. I could tell by her look of astonishment that Jenna was impressed. A growing crowd of gawkers seemed as impressed as she was.

My display of skill ate up a lot of ground, and we soon found ourselves near Stewart and Ann. He warned me to take it down a notch, but I ignored him and danced on. When the song ended, Jenna wiped the sweat from her forehead. She said she really needed to sit down for a while to recover. I have that effect on people.

We found our seats, sipped warm watery soda, watched the dancers and listened as the beach music blared. We put our heads close together and talked as best we could. She smelled terrific.

"Do you know how to shag?" Jenna breathed in my ear.

"Of *course* I do." I knew that was stupid before it was all the way out. "Uh, well . . . I sorta do, I'm just a little fuzzy on how it all goes together while dancing with someone else. Stewart says I dance like I'm dyslexic."

She giggled in my ear. "Let me teach you. Come on. It's *easy.*"

She took my hand just as "My Girl" by the Temptations came on. Jenna started counting, a concept new to me, at least as it applied to dance. "One, two, three-and-four, and fiiiiiiiive, six. On the five count, Jenna sang the word rocking back as she did. I guess I was supposed to rock too but I ended up jamming my knee into her knee and she sang, "Oooouch."

"Take it easy, Joe," Jenna squeezed my hand. She had deep brown eyes. "Relax a little. Don't work so hard. Try to *feel* the music."

I had no idea in hell what *feeling* the music meant, but I must have started to get the hang of it because Jenna kept counting and when she got to fiiiiiiive, she opened her mouth, closed her eyes and sang out the word.

"You're starting to get the hang of it, Joe," Jenna said. "Now we should try those same steps, but back-to-front this time." She turned her back to me and I took hold of her like she showed me, and we danced close enough to frustrate the Holy Ghost. She taught me how to spin. I never did get the fancy footwork down, but after several dances under Jenna's instruction, I felt like a pro.

Across the dance floor, I watched as a guy slid his date between his legs. It was a cool move. I pointed them out to Jenna and asked if she was game, and she sure was.

We did the normal steps smoothly, then I took one of Jenna's hands, whirled her around, threw one leg over her and grabbed her free hand as she lay flat on her back, waiting for me to pull her through my legs, which was just what I tried to do. This turned out to be harder than it looked.

I was off-balance, my foot slipped as I pulled, and Jenna didn't slide through my legs hardly at all. I drew her partly up, but then I lost my balance and my grip. She landed on the floor, and I landed spread eagle on top of her.

Out of nowhere, a hard spray of cold water slapped my face. Through the shower I got a foggy glimpse of a strange woman standing over me shaking a fresh bottle of seltzer and getting ready to let fly again. *What the hell?* More water squirted in my face. The woman dropped her bottle, grabbed hold of me by my armpits and jerked me to my feet.

"Gayle!" screamed Jenna, "What are you doing?"

"I was warned about you two!" She shook me and glared at Stewart.

"I can explain!" I squeaked but she squeezed harder and it *hurt*.

"Put him down!" a new voice called. "Put him down, Gayle."

It was Vicki, my sister. *Vicki? My sister?*

"This gets stranger by the minute," Stewart said.

Gayle roasted me with another hostile look, and then stared hard at Vicki. After a moment, recognition dawned on her face

"Vicki?" Gayle took a step toward my sister. "It's been a while . . ."

"You two *know* each other?"

Vicki nodded as she and Gayle left the dance floor. We followed, dumbfounded and curious. *What the hell just happened here?*

Gayle and Vicki found our table. Gayle, it turned out, was the Smithfield girls' older and much stronger sister.

"Mom sent me to spy on you," Gayle told her sisters.

"And my mom sent *me* to spy on them, too," Vicki said.

"Why spy on us?" Jenna asked. I cringed, hoping

Vicki wouldn't say. Instead, Gayle spoke up.

"Mama told you before you left," Gayle said. "She doesn't think too highly of Mrs. Baroody."

Vicki laughed. "Mama told me to go and make sure you and Stewart didn't get taken advantage of."

Jenna, Ann, Stewart and I guffawed.

"And you *agreed*?" I demanded.

"How could I not?" she laughed wickedly.

None of this made sense.

I turned to Jenna. "Your mother *knows* my mother?"

Ann spoke up. "Our mother thinks your mother is ...odd."

"*Odd*?" I said. "How odd? Odd how?"

"Oh, Joe, come *on*." Vicki rolled her eyes.

"What?" I knew, of course, but that was all supposed to be, well, *private*, I thought.

Ann looked at me curiously. "Does your mom *really* talk to the dead?" Stewart spit out his drink. "One day our dad was gassing up a boat and he overheard two ladies from Florence talking about some meeting they went to at the Baroody's, where they talked to spirits of the dead."

"Well," I said, "it's not like . . . it's not *that* bad." It was that bad. "She tries to talk to Kin, her dad, who died a while back. She thinks he has a message for her from the Beyond, an important message that . . . okay. All right. I admit it. She's a little weird."

"That's putting it mildly," Steward whispered.

Vicki slapped him on the arm.

"Wait a minute. I'm confused," I said and turned first to Gayle. "You're here because your mama wanted you to spy on us. And you're here," I said, pointing my finger at my sister, "because Mama wanted you to spy on us?"

Vicki shook her head and eyed Gayle. They shared a "see-what-I'm-up-against?" look.

Technically, Mama sent me to spy on *them*." She looked at Jenna and then Ann. "No offense meant, girls, but you are real young and real pretty, and that makes you real *dangerous*, by our mother's lights."

"She thinks you're . . ." Stewart began.

"*Sluts*, right?" Jenna said. Stewart nodded.

"That's because of me," Gayle said.

"No, it's not," Jenna said. "It's because our mother dresses like she's a teenager."

"Yeah, well," Jenna said, "our mom is weirder than just that."

"Not so weird," Gayle said. "Over-protective, maybe, after what happened to me."

"What happened to you?" Stewart blurted it out before I could.

"*Stewart!*" Vicki snarled.

"No, it's okay," Gayle said.

"It most certainly is *not* okay." Vicki looked daggers at Stewart.

"I'm not ashamed." Gayle turned to Stewart. "I got pregnant when I was sixteen. Don't get me wrong, Meg is a great daughter and I can't imagine a world without her, but I dropped out of high school and never graduated. I had planned to go to college."

She looked at me with a sheepish grin. "Sorry about spraying you, Joe."

"Anybody who dances like Joe," Stewart said, "needs a good hosing-down now and then."

Gayle nodded at Vicki. "What do you say we leave these kids alone?" She got to her feet and my sister did too. "I think they'll be okay."

The next morning Stewart and I had *another* date with the Smithfield girls, this one at the lakeside church service. I wanted to see Jenna again. Stewart wanted to see Ann again but was still weighing the risk of stirring Mama's wrath. But Mama said not a word as I broke the news and pushed a sputtering Stewart quickly out the back door.

At the lake, we spotted Ann and Jenna, and set up our lawn chairs on either side of them. Jenna leaned over to talk in my ear. She smelled like shampoo.

"I had a really nice time last night," she said.

"Me too. Thanks for the shag lessons."

Mrs. Smithfield came on the scene, and instinctively I stood up. Stewart did, too. She was a large woman, a fact emphasized by the neon green capri pants she wore and the tight white tank top. Printed in lavender across her expansive breasts was the word "*Amazing.*" I could not dispute that. Barely visible under the cantilever of her breasts was the word "*Grace.*"

"Nice outfit," Stewart said.

I could feel Mrs. Smithfield sizing us up. She tapped her temple next to her left eye and used the same finger to point at us. *I've got my eye on you.*

Mrs. Smithfield made her way to her husband.

"We both have weird moms," Jenna whispered warmly in my ear.

"That's for sure," I whispered warmly into hers.

The service was about to begin when Gayle showed up with her daughter Meg in tow. Gayle placed her chair beside Mrs. Smithfield and sat down. Meg climbed into her grandmother's lap.

It was a nice service, I suppose. I wasn't paying much attention. Instead, I watched Meg snuggle and fall asleep in her grandmother's lap, her head buried in grace. Later, after the service, Meg hopped off her grandma's lap and trotted over to get hugs from Jenna and Ann.

Meg had big eyes and a generous sprinkling of freckles on her nose. Her dark hair was bobbed summer-short. She didn't say much, but she took my hand when I extended it and curtsied.

I'm pretty sure that curtsy was the first and only one I've ever received.

I guess it's a lost art these days.

# 10

## *My Night with Ray the Cabdriver*

I stood on the curb and wildly waved my hands above my head to hail a cab at Dulles Airport in Washington, D.C., just like Mama showed me.

My mother had the only son in Florence, S.C., to be booted out of the Boy Scouts for failing to advance beyond the rank of tenderfoot, which required only the reciting of the Boy Scout Oath. To advance meant I had to go off somewhere by myself and find my own way back. It was that last part that gave me the trouble, thus Mama's detailed instructions.

"To hail a cab," she said, "stand on the curb and wave your hands." She demonstrated this by fluttering her hands back and forth above her head. "When a cab stops, you tell the driver to take you to the Capitol Building. The Congressional Office Building is connected to it. Room 312. That's where you want to go." She wrote all this out on a piece of paper and stuffed it in my shirt pocket.

I was in town on that spring day in 1973 to start a month-long internship with Congressman Ed Young of South Carolina. Apparently Mama's instructions were good, because sure enough, a yellow cab pulled up to the curb right where I stood. I put the paper back in my pocket, tossed my suitcase in the rear seat and followed it in.

"Take me to the Capitol Building," I told the driver

and glanced at my watch. "The Congressional Office Building. Congressman Ed Young's office. I need to be there before five o'clock. Room 312."

"Sure thing," the cabbie said and got the car going. Once we were out in the heavy traffic, he chuckled and said over his shoulder, "You know, to be straight with you, I'm not exactly sure how to get there."

"You don't know how to get to the *Capitol*?!"

*What are the odds? A million cab drivers in D.C., and I find the one who can't find the Capitol.*

"I'd think that would be the first question on the cab-driver test," I said.

"Whoa, take it easy, man," he laughed. "I'm a Maryland cabby. You want a D.C. cab."

So just because "Maryland" was painted in large red letters on the side of the cab, he thought I knew this.

"But hey, man, don't worry. We got plenty of time. We'll find it. Think of it as an adventure."

It turns out that in D.C., just because you can see your destination doesn't mean you know how to get there. We stopped for directions three times, and with some slick driving, we got there with ten minutes to spare.

"Wait for me, will you?" I called and jumped out of the cab, leaving my suitcase behind as collateral. I took the front steps two at a time, rushed inside and caught the elevator to the third floor. I wandered down several hallways and finally found the office – locked. My heart sank. Not a good beginning at all.

Dejected and back outside, I looked for the cab, but it was gone. *Great. The guy had ripped me off.*

Then I realized I'd left by the wrong door. A Capitol cop let me back in and led me to the right exit. I could see the cabdriver leaning against his yellow cab in the sunlight, hands clasped behind his neck, watching the clouds roll by. As I came down the stairs, he saw me.

"Too late, huh?" he said.

"Too late."

"No dough?" he said after a moment.

I shook my head. "Not enough."

"Hey, man, don't take it personal. It's all cool. Treat yourself to a deep breath."

He took his own advice. I did too and felt a little better.

"What am I gonna do?" I said more to myself than to him.

The cabby slapped me soundly on the back and gave me a wide smile.

"Tell you what," he said. "The meter says seven-fifty. Call it ten bucks, and you can bunk with me tonight. On top of that, I'll feed you and get you back here early in the morning, *tout de suite.*"

"But . . ." I was puzzled. "You don't even know me."

"Don't I? Well, man, you look like a nice enough guy who's havin' himself a bad day. Let me give you a hand. Think of it as an adventure."

"You said that before."

"I like adventure."

I looked at him for the first time, really. He was a hippie, late twenties, with the standard scruffy beard and long, scraggly hair pulled tight into a ponytail. His clothes were plain and clean, his hands scrubbed. He had an open face and merry eyes and crow's feet when he smiled.

"Sure. Why not?" I opened the door and climbed in the front seat. Off to Maryland we went.

"Ray Rogers," he said and put out his hand. I gave him mine, and we shook.

While we drove, we swapped notes. I told him I was a junior at USC in Columbia, South Carolina, in Washington for the internship. I wanted to experience politics first-hand, I said, to see it up close. I said I hoped to sit in on the Watergate Hearings, and we talked about that for a while.

Ray told me he'd dropped out of college, avoided the draft, and opposed the war, and thought USC was in California. He said he lived with his girlfriend, Janet, and their six-month-old daughter, Ray-Jan.

"Don't know that I've ever heard that name," I said.

"It's a hyphenated name, man. You know, it puts together Ray and Janet. Fits her well. She hollers a lot, even when she's happy."

"This is pretty short notice. You sure Janet won't mind me staying?"

"Yeah, man," Ray grinned. "We lived in a commune for a couple of years. That's where I met her. Togetherness, man. Like the song says, man, we all got to help each other if we're gonna get by, right?" He paused. "Say, you like basketball? USA plays Russia tonight. We'll grill some burgers and watch the game."

"Sounds great," I said.

At their apartment, Ray introduced me to Janet. She was a few years younger than Ray, petite, with long, straight brunette hair that fell to her waist. Ray-Jan, true to her billing, began screaming the second she saw me.

"It takes her a little while to warm up to strangers," Janet assured me.

We ate burgers and salad while Steppenwolf's "Born to be Wild" blared from the phonograph. Apparently it was among Ray-Jan's favorites.

The TV was in their bedroom on a dresser, facing a king-sized waterbed that took up most of the room. I had never seen a real waterbed. Radical furniture was slow to show up in South Carolina. Ray adjusted the television antennae. He wore a t-shirt bearing a large peace sign and gold silk pajama pants.

When he got the picture right, he dove onto the waterbed and rocked with the ripples.

"Jump in, man," he said. I eased myself onto the bed backwards, and Ray bounced on the bladder hard enough to tip me onto my back. I laughed and rolled around for a while, finally landing next to him near the head of the bed. *Boy, if Mama could see me now.*

Janet came in wearing gray sweatpants and the top of Ray's silk pajamas. She handed Ray-Jan to me, and on cue the baby began crying. Janet wiggled in between us and got comfortable. After a few minutes with the baby, I realized she wasn't really crying, just noisy. They let her holler. About ten minutes into the first half, Janet took the baby and she fell right to sleep.

At halftime, Ray went to the kitchen to pop some popcorn, and Ray-Jan woke up fussing.

"Now, now," Janet cooed. "Somebody's hungry."

"Let me get the bottle," I volunteered and struggled to hoist myself off the bed.

"No need, Joe," Janet said.

I started to say it was no bother, but no words came out as I watched her unbutton her top and arrange herself.

"I'm the bottle," she said sweetly and put Ray-Jan where she wanted to be.

"Well, sure, I . . . I mean, of course . . . you, uh . . . are." I had never so much as thought about talking with a woman my own age who was breastfeeding her baby. I had no idea what to say, and so I stuttered and stared. My mouth may have fallen open. I could hear Mama's voice in my head saying, *Joe, what the hell are you doing in bed with a hippie cabdriver and his breastfeeding wife and baby?*

I was suddenly sweaty and felt like a blinking traffic light. Janet smiled serenely and went about her business. Somehow that made things worse, and I was suddenly overcome by the need to flee, and so I did. I bolted for the door and ran smack into Ray. I hit him head-to-head and sent him and his gigantic bowl of popcorn flying. For a moment, it looked like snow in the bedroom, and I slipped out and away. Behind me Janet and Ray laughed long and loud, and maybe the baby did too.

I spent the night on the couch, pretending to be asleep. Ray and Janet respected my space, tiptoeing around and talking in whispers like they thought I was sleeping.

When Ray came in the next morning, I was already dressed and ready to go. On the way to Congressman

Young's office, he bought me breakfast. And then he politely refused to take the money I owed him.

"Nah, man, you keep it. No worries." He looked at me intently. "You're okay now. When I saw you yesterday, you had this kind of desperate look. I figured what the hell, you know? Do unto others as you would have them do unto you. That's the rule, man."

"You read the Bible?" I sounded astonished.

"Yeah, I do sometimes." He smiled and gave me his business card. "It's all about us, man, us together in this world. Togetherness. You never know when some lost soul will need some help. Last night it was you. Tonight it could be me. We got to help each other if we're gonna get by." I had nothing to add to that, so I grinned and gave him my hand. He shook it, then pulled me close for a bear hug and another slap on the back. He climbed back into his taxi and waved.

"Sorry about the bump on your forehead," I said and rubbed my own swollen brow.

"I'm not," he said with a big laugh. "Every real adventure leaves a scar."

I never saw Ray again, but I saved his card.

Later that summer, back in South Carolina, I was speeding down the back roads on my way to Santee Lake. Up ahead, traffic was slowing down to go around a car that was stalled on the side of the road. An elderly black man stood beside the car, waving a white handkerchief, but it was like he wasn't even there. Stopping for black people on the side of the road wasn't something respectable white

Southerners did in 1973. As I drove by, I saw a look on the man's face, one I recognized. I hesitated a moment, then pulled off the road and backed up.

"Need help?" I called.

"Yes, I sure do," the man said. "I got lost and ran out of gas. I was supposed to meet my relatives two hours ago."

"How 'bout a lift?" I said. "I've got a gas can in the trunk, and there's a gas station a few miles up the road. It has a pay phone. I'll give you a lift, if you like."

"I would like that fine."

He opened the passenger door and paused to pound the dust from his clothes.

"I'm Mike White," he said and slid into the front seat. "I really appreciate this."

"Joe Baroody," I said. A flash of discomfort coursed through me as he shut the door and settled into the front seat. Back then, blacks weren't supposed to ride up front.

At the gas station, he called his relatives while I filled the gas can. We returned to his car, and I poured the gasoline into the tank for him. He thanked me again and gave me his business card, which read, *Mike A. White Sr., Bartender, Bronx, N.Y.* With the card he also gave me a hundred-dollar bill.

His gesture caught me completely off guard. A black man, tipping me a hundred dollars! When I felt myself sputtering, I heard Ray's voice. "You never know when some lost soul may need your help."

"Thank you, Mister White," I said and gave the bill back. "But it's not necessary."

"You sure, son?" he asked kindly. "Don't know what I'd have done if you hadn't come along."

"Yes sir, I'm sure. Been lost a time or two myself."

"Well, thanks again, son. If you're ever in the Bronx, give me a call. I make a mean martini."

"I'll do that, sir. But I don't ever plan to be in the Bronx any time soon."

"Plans change. I didn't plan to get lost on the back roads of South Carolina."

I never saw Mike or Ray again. But their cards hold the place of Matthew 7:12 in my Bible, the Golden Rule.

# 11

## *Hi, Jordan*

The housekeeper stuffed the trash into the bag on her pushcart and then swept her dust mop under one of the incubators. She paused to give her arthritic knees a rest. Across the neonatal intensive care unit, a young mother perched on a stool and peered into an isolette. Inside, her baby lay motionless, tubes and wires extending in all directions.

A nurse walked in quietly and inspected the tubes, wires and machines.

"Jordan is comfortable," she said and patted the mother's shoulder. The mother looked up and nodded. Her face was blank, her eyes empty.

"Thanks," she whispered.

The nurse moved on to the next isolette.

The housekeeper gradually worked her mop and push-cart to the young mother. She leaned on her mop handle and watched the infant for a moment.

"Your first?"

The mother looked up and nodded. The housekeeper gave her a sympathetic smile.

"I've got three teens of my own. They drive me crazy, but thank God they're all healthy."

"Jordan came last night," the mother whispered in a voice as thin as paper. "The doctor says there's some brain problem." She shook her head and looked back at Jordan. "But doctors can be wrong, can't they?"

The housekeeper stood quietly looking down at the baby. About six pounds, she judged. Maybe full term. A thin breathing tube ran into the infant's mouth. A tube in the scalp supplied fluids. Wires from tiny heart monitor patches ran to a bank of blinking machines.

The mother pointed to one of the machines. "That one there keeps Jordan breathing. If there's no improvement in twenty-four hours, the doctor says we'll probably have to unplug it and let my baby die."

"Do you have family?" the housekeeper asked. The mother nodded.

"They're on their way. Be here in the morning." Tears ran down her cheeks. "I don't have a husband."

The housekeeper gave the mother's shoulder a squeeze.

"My first was a stillborn," the housekeeper said. She took in a deep breath and let it out slowly. "Like I said, I've got three healthy ones, all good kids, but it doesn't make up for the one I lost. He'd be 18 now. I think of him every day." She took a tissue for herself and handed one to the mother.

"Goodness, child," the housekeeper said. "You must be awfully uncomfortable on that hard stool. Let me get you a real chair." She rested her mop against the wall and left. She was back in a few minutes, pushing a rocking chair with a cushioned seat. The mother sat down.

"That's much better. Thank you." She dabbed her eyes with the tissue, then turned her attention back to Jordan. The housekeeper went back to her mopping.

The nurse returned, checking baby and machines again. Satisfied, she squatted beside the unmoving mother and squeezed her hand.

"Would you like to hold Jordan?"

"Can I? It's okay?" The mother's face lit up in a smile. "It won't hurt?"

"Not a bit." She opened the top of the isolette, carefully rearranged the wires and tubes, and gently passed baby to mother.

"Hi, Jordan," the mother said sweetly through her sniffles. "I'm your mama, and I love you."

She smiled a big smile and tenderly kissed all ten fingers and all ten toes. She held her baby against her breast and sighed, closed her eyes, and began to rock. In moments, her face softened.

The nurse and the housekeeper watched from the nurse's station.

"It's so sad," the housekeeper said. "That baby won't make it through the night."

"Sure, it's sad. But this is a good thing right now. That little mother is on a better path through her dark days ahead. She got to hug her baby. She got to know her baby just a little bit. She got to rock her baby to sleep. That counts."

They watched the young mother stroke Jordan's head and softly brush the baby's cheek with hers.

# 12

## *Hush Hour*

On Tuesdays I got Mac and Blakely ready for school so my wife, who worked the three to eleven p.m. shift as a nurse, could have a few extra hours of sleep. Also on Tuesdays, I attended an 8:30 a.m. contemplative prayer group that spent part of its time in complete silence and stillness before God.

"Breakfast is ready. Hurry up. Get moving. Daddy's got to go pray!"

I said this while exuberantly singing "Swing Low, Sweet Chariot." I didn't know which they disliked more – my singing or the song.

I had put together a good breakfast of frozen waffles and Pepsi that the kids seemed to like. This morning Mac spilled his drink and Blakely threw a fit when I failed to cut her waffle into perfect squares. To make matters worse, Mac refused to brush his teeth. Then Blakely, complaining that I'd put her dress on backwards (it looked fine to me), woke Nancy to report my ineptitude.

We'd almost made it out the door when Nancy called out, "Mac? Did you change your underwear?" He did sometimes wear the same pair for days. He claimed I once told him it was okay, but I do not remember that.

"Did you?" I asked. His blush said he didn't.

What we had was a moral dilemma, and time was short.

"Just tell her you did," I whispered. He did, and we left.

I hurried the kids to the car, got in and realized I had forgotten the keys.

"Damn," I said. Immediately, Blakely's hand appeared in front of me, palm up. I owed her a dollar – payoff for saying a bad word.

I rang the bell, and my wife opened the door, clearly not happy.

"Sorry. Forgot my keys."

Nancy picked up the keys from the table near the door. "Did *you* change your underwear?" She handed me the keys, then swung the door closed.

"Of course," I called through the door.

I hurried back to the car, started it up and shot out the driveway, causing Blakely and Mac to slide sideways as I turned around. With my focus on taking every advantage I could – going for the open lanes, rushing through yellow lights – I did not talk, except to the traffic when it got in my way.

"I hate Tuesdays," Mac said as I pulled up in front of the school. "You make us rush too much on Tuesdays."

"Hurry along," I said. As soon as the door closed, I veered back into traffic, bound for prayer group and quiet contemplation. At the intersection just before the entrance to the church, the light turned yellow as I neared it. I gunned the accelerator, congratulating myself on making it through the red without getting caught. As I entered the church parking lot, I saw an open space right at the entrance. I glided in and threw the gearshift into park as I came to a full stop. I jumped out of the car and bounded up the steps. The door was locked. A slip of notepaper was taped above the handle. *No Entrance,* it read. *A time of silence is being observed. "Be still and know God" (Psalm 46:10)*

"Damn!"

In my mind's eye, Blakely's hand appeared in front of me, palm up. And I heard Mac say, "I hate Tuesdays. You make us rush too much on Tuesdays."

# 13

## *True Concessions*

Drive-in movies were a centerpiece of the social scene in 1970. As was our habit, my date and I tried to get us both in for the price of one. I would get in the trunk of the 1968 fastback Torino my father allowed me to use while my date drove and paid a single dollar for a single ticket. When she parked the car, I'd clamber out of the trunk and slide into the passenger seat.

One night, rather than putting me in the trunk, we decided to try something new. She squeezed herself down onto the floorboard and worked the gas and brake pedals with her hands. We had a wonderful time driving down the highway on our way to the movie. I stuck my leg out the window and waved to passing motorists with my foot, certain they were as impressed with me as I was with myself. It was ultimately unsurprising that our front end wound up in the back end of a pickup truck. Nobody was hurt, but it was a hard lesson about honesty, responsibility and morality.

Since that hard lesson, I've become an ordained minister, a husband and a father of two. I see myself as honest, responsible and moral. But on a Friday night, when my children were young, another movie-going experience taught me I still had a lot to learn.

By then the drive-in had long since been replaced

by a multi-cinema theater, my girlfriend by my wife, my dad's Torino with a forty-eight-month loan and my youth with parenthood. I arrived home after a full day's work and was greeted at the door by my children, Mac, seven, and Blakely, four. Looking at me with eyes big and brown, they pleaded with me to take them to the movies. I was determined to rebut their begging with a show of strict parental authority. I explained that I was tired after working for God all day, that it was late and that going to the movies cost a small fortune. They listened patiently but were unimpressed and named the movie they wanted to see. Looking for an out, I said, "Maybe Mama has something for me to do."

"Enjoy the movie," Nancy called.

I surrendered and searched through the refrigerator for a soft drink to sneak into the show. It was wrong, and I knew it, but times were tough. This wasn't 1970, after all, and movie food didn't come cheap. God certainly could not want me to eat popcorn without a drink. He would understand.

My children were of tender years, and I didn't want to involve them in this. Such complicated ethical decisions were best handled by a qualified adult. But I was unable to escape my daughter's watchful eye.

"What are you doing?" she asked.

"Just looking around."

"For what?"

"It's time to go! Get moving!"

She saw the drink in my hand. "What are you getting that for?"

"Well, I . . . I just thought I would take one to the movie."

"You're not supposed to do that, are you?"

"Well, technically, no, but it's okay to do it tonight."

"Oh, boy! Can I do it, too?"

"No, no. This is just for adults, not children."

"If you can do it, why can't I?"

"You'll understand these things one day, when you're older. I'll buy you a drink, but you mustn't tell anyone I'm bringing mine into the movie. It'll be our secret."

I then explained my devious plan to my son, telling him I needed his jacket to hide my drink. It's always good to make the kids feel like they're part of any project.

At the theater, I again emphasized the need for secrecy. The soda can was in my jacket pocket. I draped my jacket over my arm and Mac's jacket over that. I was prepared. My children understood their orders. We were ready for the first test: the ticket booth.

While paying for our tickets, I managed to let both jackets slide off my arm, and the can hit the floor with a thud. The man taking tickets stared at me. Sweat trickled down my back. He said nothing.

But Blakely did.

"Is the drink okay, Daddy?" Her question rang out with the authority of E. F. Hutton. Everyone in the theater stopped and turned their eyes to me.

Next was the concession counter. While I bought popcorn and drinks for the kids, the soda can slipped once again, this time banging against the glass counter.

I grabbed my knee, feigned a pained look and flashed a stern glare at my children to remind them of our code of silence. The girl behind the counter asked if I was all right. I smiled, nodded and limped away, clutching my popcorn and the jacket with the contraband.

I advised the kids of proper popcorn procedure and the importance of waiting until the movie started to begin eating, an admonishment they acknowledged by nodding their heads as they munched on their popcorn and sipped their drinks. Meanwhile, I kept my drink under wraps. The ticket booth and candy counter were behind me. I had conquered the enemy.

"Daddy, have you opened your drink yet?" Blakely called out, just as one of the previews ended. I gave her a thumbs up, then glanced down our aisle and was grateful to find that our neighbors appeared inattentive.

The movie began. I popped the top on the soda.

It exploded. Foamy cola spewed everywhere. Frantically, I slurped the overflow, but the foam fizzed up into my nostrils and I sprayed out a loud sneeze. Mac and Blakely laughed loudly. Our neighbors were not amused.

As things settled down, I ate my popcorn and started in on what was left of my drink, confident I had gotten away with it. Ten minutes into the movie, the screen went dark, the lights came on and scratching came from the speakers. I went cold. This was it. I'd been caught. They probably knew all along. They were waiting to catch me in the act of consuming the smuggled soda. Any second, FBI agents would run down the aisle, throw me to the floor, frisk and handcuff me. I looked for the exits.

My life was over. My kids would be fatherless, my wife a prison widow. I had fallen from grace as a minister.

From the speakers, a calm voice said that, due to a small fire in a nearby store, everyone would have to evacuate the theater.

My kids got up to leave and saw me frozen to my seat, soda can clenched firmly in my hand.

"It's okay, Dad." Mac was unruffled. "Let's go." He took me by the hand, pulled me from my seat, and led me from the theater. Once outside, my children stood in front of me.

"I hope you learned your lesson," Blakely said, squinching her face.

"I'm sorry," I said. "I won't do that again."

We held hands as we walked to the car.

"We won't tell Mom" Mac said.

"Not this time," added Blakely.

# 14

## *Little Boys and Mamas*

"I want to have this," Mama said, passing me an article that touted a miraculous new surgery. We were sitting at her kitchen table on that June morning. A five-year battle with emphysema had confined my mother to a wheelchair. A nasal oxygen cannula breathed life into her diseased lungs. Since my father's death three months earlier, she had steadily declined and now, at seventy, she was desperate.

I thought the article was from the *National Enquirer*, her main source of inspiration, but I was wrong. It was written by a *New York Times* reporter and had been picked up by *The State* newspaper. It told of doctors in St. Louis and Dallas who had eased emphysema symptoms by surgically removing lung damage. It was not a cure but, if successful, allowed emphysema sufferers to take a deep breath. One seventy-six-year-old patient had returned to playing golf three times a week, the story said. My mother's illness, however, was more advanced, with additional complications from taking steroid medications.

She was ready to try anything. After several examinations, she was referred to the medical center in Dallas, where she was accepted as a high-risk candidate. We arranged for a medical transport jet to fly my mother and me to the center. I would stay with her during the week of preliminary testing and the surgery itself. Then my older sister Vicki would relieve me. If all went according to plan, Mama would return home in three to four weeks, able to take a deep breath.

On that day in August, Vicki, my wife Nancy and younger brother Kenny piled into the back seat of our brand new Cadillac. My father had purchased it for Mama shortly after he was diagnosed with lung cancer. He drove it only once, and my mother never drove it, owing to their health issues. As the child who lived close, driving them around had been my job. I settled in behind the wheel while Mama, sitting next to me, looked straight ahead. Her portable canister hissed as it released oxygen.

"Let's get moving," she said.

When I was six, Mama took me to the circus. She clutched my hand tightly as we made our way through the crowd to our seats. We must have walked twenty yards before I looked up and realized that the hand I was holding was not hers. Terrified, I began to run. "Mama! Mama!" I cried. Suddenly she appeared in the midst of the crowd and swept me up in her arms. I clung to her neck, sobbing. I felt that fear again as I drove to the airport. I patted her on the knee.

"You okay?"

She managed a weak smile and nodded.

But anyone watching us board the jet that morning would have thought I was the patient. I do not like flying. The act of walking into the airport made me dizzy. As I made my way slowly up the steps into the jet, I gulped downed the rest of my Dramamine tablets. Mama, though, displayed a strange burst of energy. A nurse helped her into the jet and asked her to lie down on the stretcher provided for patients. Mama refused.

"Joe might need it," she said in a strong voice. "Flying sometimes upsets his tummy." She sat in the upright seat next to the stretcher and ordered me and the nurse to take the only remaining seat, a bench located directly behind her.

"Notify me immediately if Joe feels sick," she commanded the nurse.

Where had this energy come from? I was baffled. But I did as I was told, assuring Mama I was fine. Satisfied that all was in order, Mama yelled out to the pilot, "It's okay to take off now."

The pilot politely acknowledged Mama's command and informed us the flight to Dallas would take a little over two hours, but because the time zone changed, we would gain back an hour. I checked my watch and it was 10:05 a.m. Eastern Standard Time. Time zones. Ecclesiastes 3 popped into my mind: "For everything there is a season, and a time for every matter under heaven: a time to be born and a time to die." The verse refers to the inevitable events – most beyond our control – that occur as time passes. A time to die: the threat of death. Maybe that explained Mama's sudden burst of energy. Another wave of fear swept through me.

The nurse beside me was in her mid-twenties and very attractive.

"You know," I said, trying for nonchalant. "I don't *really* have a problem flying. Mama just likes to carry on. I don't know what's gotten into her. She treats me like I'm a child." The nurse had auburn hair, deep brown eyes and a smooth, pale face flecked with freckles. An expensive ring glittered on her finger. Her looks reminded me of the photograph of Mama that I knew so well. It was taken when she was in nursing school. In the photograph, Mama's hair was auburn, and her skin was pale, smooth and lovely, too.

"Mama, she was a nurse until she married Daddy. Daddy was an obstetrician-gynecologist. He died a few months ago. My wife," I said, "you might have noticed her at the airport. She was the one with the dark hair. She's a nurse, too, just like you. Her name's Nancy. My sister is a nurse. She was at the airport, too. By the way, what's your name?"

"Angela," she said. "Sorry to hear about your dad."

"Thanks. Angela. Nice name." I pointed at her ring. "Engaged or married?"

"Engaged," she said. She had a nice smile and very nice teeth. "The wedding is the end of September." She held out the ring so I could see it. I took her hand and admired the ring and its rock. Her hand was warm and soft. She took it away while I was still holding it.

I cleared my throat.

"Nancy and I, we met at McLeod Hospital in Florence," I said. "She had just graduated. I was an orderly then.

Joe, that's my name. 'Joe the Orderly,' they called me. I could insert a suppository with either hand."

"Oh. Well." She made a face. "That's . . . nice."

I hurried on. "Eventually I became a chaplain at that hospital. It's McLeod Regional now. Now I'm a pastoral psychotherapist." I use that term when I want to seem important and mysterious.

"Oh, I've worked with chaplains." She seemed unimpressed. "I worked ER in Atlanta. You guys were all over the place."

I was about to defend my profession when Mama interrupted.

"Joe, are you okay?" she called. "Tummy all right? Angela, you watch him. He fidgets when his tummy's upset. You watch him. And Joe, you quit flirting with her."

I looked at Angela and rolled my eyes.

"Mama, I'm fine. I wasn't flirting." Oh, yes I was. "We're just talking. You should get some rest. Are you sure you don't want to lie down?"

"I do better sitting up. You might need the stretcher."

I turned back to Angela, my ears burning.

"Angela," I said. "What a pretty name."

"Thanks. Again."

"Oh, yeah. Sorry." The ears were burning worse. I dropped my voice to a whisper. "I don't know what to do with Mama. She was real quiet and tired-like on the way to the airport. Now she acts like she's not even sick. She must have reverted to the denial state. Are you familiar with Elizabeth Kubler-Ross's five stages of dying?"

"Yes, I am," she said, again unimpressed. "I think your

mom is just nervous, and maybe a little scared. Maybe you are, too. Why don't you try to rest? Maybe read a magazine."

I got the message. It was time to settle down. Rest or read? Reading would certainly give me motion sickness, so it had to be rest. I unbuckled my seatbelt to get more comfortable, but when I buckled back up I somehow pinched the tip of my finger in the mechanism. I reflexively shook my hand then stuck my finger in my mouth and sucked. Angela thumbed through a magazine, showing no concern. My finger was fine, but inspecting it brought to mind a memory.

In 1956, when I was four, standing on the crossbar of my swing set inspecting the hinge that moved the horsey back and forth, I stuck the middle finger of my right hand inside the hinge and pushed. A searing pain shot through my body. I fell to the ground and screamed. Blood was all over my hand. The hinge had sliced off my fingertip. Terrified, I ran into the house still screaming. Mama and Vicki were in the den watching TV. I thrust my finger in Mama's face. She grabbed me and rushed me to the bathroom, where she ran cold water over my hand and poured alcohol over my finger, making me scream even louder. She wrapped my hand in a towel and called Daddy, who was working at the hospital. Back in the den, she rocked me until Daddy arrived.

A surgeon grafted my finger to my abdomen so the skin there would attach itself to my fingertip. The newly created fingertip turned out to be a rather unpleasant looking little bump. When puberty set in years later, sprouts of fine hair grew out of the fingertip.

"Ever see a hairy fingertip?" I wiggled mine under Angela's nose.

She jerked back. "What is *that*?"

This caught Mama's attention. "What's going on?"

"Nothing, Mama," I said. "I was just showing Angela my hairy finger."

"For God's sake, Joe. Stop it. You know better than that. Angela, don't mind Joe. He always thought girls were impressed by it. No girl ever was. Most reacted like you did." I did not know Mama knew about all that.

"Please show me your engagement ring," she said to Angela. "I heard you say you were getting married in September." Angela unbuckled her seatbelt and kneeled down beside Mama. Apparently her engagement ring was more interesting than my hairy finger.

We still had more than an hour to go. I leaned my head back and closed my eyes. Mama asked Angela about her wedding plans and then began to explain correct wedding etiquette. Mama gave her opinions as though they were indisputable facts, and she had an opinion about everything. Like the time when I was six and she decided I should play Small Fry Baseball. After watching me play in pickup games in the backyard, she decided it was time for organized ball. But competition in a real game scared me, so I quit.

Mama was not pleased. "Only cowards quit," she said. I wasn't sure what that meant but it didn't sound good. By the age of nine, I was more confident and signed up for

Dixie Youth Baseball. I advanced through Pony League, high school and American Legion baseball. Mama never attended a game.

"Angela," Mama said. "Is Joe all right? Ask him about his tummy." I spoke up and assured Mama I was fine. This time she persisted. "Angela, get him a Coke and some saltines."

I surrendered and accepted the snack, which was a huge mistake. Within a few minutes of downing the Coke, my "tummy" was telling me I needed a lavatory. Caffeine and already jumpy nerves don't mix well. We had only twenty minutes left in the air, and I hoped I could hold out. I crossed my legs, clamped my knees together and adjusted my seatbelt. Nothing helped.

"Something wrong?" Angela asked.

"No," I said. "I'm fine. Seatbelt's just a little tight, that's all."

"You sure? You don't look fine."

"Really, I'm okay. Nothing's wrong."

"Is he squirming?" Mama asked loud enough for the pilot to hear.

"Why, yes," Angela said. "Quite a bit."

I shut my eyes, gritted my teeth and clamped the knees tighter. I dreaded the next words out of Mama's mouth.

"If he's squirming," she said, "that means he has to tee-tee. On long trips we always had to take along a Mason jar. Whenever our little Joe started squirming, we got out the Mason jar because we knew he had to tee-tee. Now Joe, let Angela help you. It's okay, she's a nurse."

A hand tapped my shoulder. I opened my eyes and Angela flashed me a smile.

"Does 'little Joe' have to tee-tee?"

I was about to bust. I couldn't speak, only nod.

"Well," she said. "I don't have a Mason jar but maybe this will do." She pulled a plastic hospital urinal from under the stretcher and handed it to me.

Mama struggled after the surgery. Vicki relieved me after a week, but I returned within a few days because Mama went into respiratory failure and was placed on a respirator. She rallied and began breathing on her own. Job demands forced Vicki and me to leave. We made arrangements for one of Mama's trusted sitters to fly out. Her condition steadily deteriorated. Mama now hardly ate and spoke only in whispers.

Six weeks later and back in Florence, I was alone in my office and lost in thought. I jumped when the phone rang. The operator announced she was connecting me with Vicki in Rock Hill and the sitter in a three-way call. Mama was near death. The sitter put the phone to Mama's ear. Vicki and I spoke goodbyes and words of love. The sitter's voice broke in. She had put her hand on Mama's chest and felt no heartbeat. I heard the heart monitor's alarm shrilling in the background. Mama was dead. I hung up the phone, folded my arms, lay my head on my desk and began to sob. This time she wasn't going to appear in the crowd and sweep me up in her arms. This time I really had lost her.

Every August I think about that flight to Dallas. When we left Florence, the clock said 10:05 a.m. When we landed in Dallas more than two hours later, the clock said only a single hour had passed. The duration of the flight had little to do with clock time, with the mere passage of time. It had everything to do with dwelling *in* time, living in the power and meaning of the moment. We were swept up in "a time to die." My mother's time came with one last burst of energy, one last chance to be Mama. And for me, the forty-two-year-old husband, father and pastoral psychotherapist, her time to die gave me one more chance to be the little boy who needed his Mama, who needed her to interrupt his flirtations with the pretty nurse, worry over his upset tummy, tell him to eat and make sure he got the Mason jar.

A time to die is a time zone unto itself, one that allows us to simply dwell, that allows middle-aged men and dying mothers to become little boys and mamas – one more time.

# 15

## *The Old Lady Who Lay Naked*

What do you say to a naked ninety-one-year-old woman who refuses to utter a single word?

"Go Cocks!" That's what I said. Steve Spurrier, the head football coach for the University of South Carolina Gamecocks, was being interviewed on ESPN, playing on the TV just over the woman's head.

The naked lady was Miss Mamie, a resident of the Presbyterian Home in Florence. Failing health had exiled her to the infirmary where, in addition to not eating or taking medication, she adamantly refused to speak.

My wife Nancy, a nurse at the infirmary, and Eleanor, a nursing assistant, were certain God had chosen me as the agent of Miss Mamie's redemption. They encouraged me to please visit her and try to get some response. I agreed and headed to meet this "Miss Mamie." I walked in and ran right back out, horrified. Nancy and Eleanor had left out the part about Miss Mamie refusing to wear clothes.

Now, after several weeks of visiting her, her nude, wrinkled body, lying spread eagle on the bed didn't cause so much as a flinch.

"You know," I said during one of my visits, "you are not my first naked lady."

Her face contorted into a curious expression. Sliding my hand under hers, I admired the burgundy nail polish Nancy had applied earlier that day. "Nope, I was fourteen when my buddies and I conned our way into the hoochie-coochie show at the fair. "Doin' the Dog" started playing, and this attractive young lady appeared on stage gyrating and slinging her clothes.

"I was honored when her tiny tasseled bra hit me in the face. My friends laughed and pushed me to the front of the stage. She grabbed my hand and pulled. Before I knew it, the naked lady and I were doin' the dog."

Miss Mamie's face twitched, and she squeezed my hand. Stories seemed to be my best hope at drawing some reaction from her. She finally spoke the night I told her about the blinking yellow caution light I had stolen.

But it was a song and not my story that drew her reaction. I was laughing at my story when I stopped and said, "You hear that?" A group of children, probably a Sunday school class, were coming down the hall singing "This Little Light of Mine." Their voices grew louder as they neared Miss Mamie's room:

*This little light of mine, I'm gonna let it shine –*
*This little light of mine, I'm gonna let it shine –*
*This little light of mine, I'm gonna let it shine –*
*Let it shine, let it shine, let it shine.*

The teacher came in, saw me with a naked Miss Mamie and quickly left. Their voices drifted down the hall. "You like that song?" I began to hum it, at first not noticing Miss Mamie's expression.

Her eyes squinted, and her lips pursed, and then she yelled, "Get the hell out!"

I jumped back, startled. "Get out," she shouted. "I hate that song! I hate it!"

I didn't know what to say. I mustered some words. "But Miss Mamie, I don't understand. What's wrong? Why don't you like that song?"

She shouted back. "I hate it! And I'm tired of you and your stupid stories. Get out. Get the hell out of here. Now!"

I pleaded, but to no avail, and so I left. The fact that she had finally spoken was little consolation, and I wondered what it was about that song that provoked such anger. I stayed away for several weeks, but Nancy told me that Miss Mamie had retreated to silence again. When she or Eleanor tried to get Miss Mamie to eat or take her medication, she spit it out. Nancy said Miss Mamie was dying.

One afternoon, Nancy called me at the office. "Joe," she said excitedly, "Miss Mamie spoke!"

"Well, I'll be," I said. "What did she say?"

"She wants to see you," Nancy said.

That evening I knocked on her door. Mamie's voice sounded like a rusty hinge when she invited me in. She was bone thin. Her long legs looked like sticks, her face gaunt. Miss Mamie patted the bed, motioning me to sit. She handed me an envelope that contained a faded photograph of eight girls. They looked to be about twelve or thirteen years old. There was a lady, probably in her thirties, standing beside them.

"That's me," Miss Mamie said, pointing to a tall girl in the middle of the back row. Even though the picture was blurred, I could see that Miss Mamie was a beauty in her day.

"We called our Sunday school class the Sunshine Girls."

Pointing to the lady, Miss Mamie said, "That's Mrs. Hooks, our teacher. The picture was taken the day she left. Turn it over." I read a note on the back aloud:

*Dear Mamie,*
*You will always be my favorite sunshine girl. Don't ever forget our song –"This Little Light of Mine." Music is your light. Let it shine before others.*
*All my love,*
*Mrs. Hooks, 1923*

"When my father got drunk, he liked to hit things smaller than him, like me and my mother. He left when I was about ten. My mother took up with a string of men. A few of them were nice to me. But more weren't. One called it lovemaking, but it didn't feel loving to me.

"The only place I felt safe and happy was with Mrs. Hooks and the Sunshine Girls. And then Mrs. Hooks left, and the Sunshine Girls were no more. I left home at sixteen and headed to New York City to become a famous singer. Instead, I got pregnant and became a waitress. My daughter left me when she was sixteen. Then I became what you called a hoochie coochie dancer."

Miss Mamie paused and looked at me. "Why Joe, I do believe you're blushing." I was.

"At first taking my clothes off in front of howling men was exciting. And there was always some lonely man waiting for me. Seemed I only tasted love when I took off my clothes. I did that until a manager fired me for being too old. I was thirty-five. I moved to Florence and worked at a Huddle House as a waitress. I never saw my daughter again."

Tears streamed down her cheeks. I tried to dab them with a Kleenex, but she turned her head. I didn't know what to say. And then it hit me.

"When Rabbi Susya lay dying," I said. "He feared what God would say to him about his miserable life. When he arrived at the Pearly Gates, God did not speak at all about the life he lived. His only comment was about the life he did not live. *'Why weren't you Susya?'* said God. *'Why did you not become what only you could become?'* The greatest despair, perhaps the greatest sin, is the unlived life."

I continued. "Miss Mamie, even at ninety-one, you still have a life to live. You can still be the *Sunshine Girl.* You can still be Mamie."

"Go now, Joe," she whispered. "Let me rest." I hesitated, reluctant to leave.

When I returned a few days later, I was as shocked as I was on my first visit when I saw her naked. This day, her bed was empty and neatly made.

"Hello Joe." Her crisp voice came from the recliner. Dressed in a nightgown and robe with burgundy nails gleaming and her thin gray hair pulled back, she smiled.

"Miss Mamie! Wow! You look so . . . so . . . *well.* I have never seen you with clothes on. I don't know what to say."

"Want to dance?"

"What? Do I want to dance?"

She rose from the recliner, placed one arm about my waist, and with the other, took my hand. As we embraced in a slow dance, she sang, *I see trees of green . . . red roses too. I see 'em bloom for me and for you. And I think to myself . . . what a wonderful world.*

She strained to hit the notes, but the words floated softly into my ears. When she stopped singing, she leaned her head against my chest. I interrupted the silence. "Did I ever tell you about the time I almost got arrested at Fat Harold's during Easter Break?"

She squeezed a little tighter and said, "Shhhh. Let's just dance. I haven't danced in a long time."

# 16

## *Maroon Cadillac*

"You coming?" Daddy said, his tone impatient. "They'll be here any minute."

"You realize you're buying a Cadillac, Daddy, not a pizza."

"A ma*roon* Cadillac," Daddy said, emphasizing the -*roon* with a purse of his lips.

"I'm on my way."

I hung up the phone and headed for his house. All my life, Daddy had always bought Pontiacs or Buicks, "pre-owned," he would say, not "used." He liked a four-year loan at a low rate and was willing to put in the time at the bank until he was satisfied. This time, though, he had his eye on a Cadillac, broken-in but still the current model, and he wanted to pay cash for it.

My father had terminal lung cancer. We learned this while he was helping my mother fight her own battle with emphysema. The Cadillac was for her, he insisted. I knew better but didn't argue.

The Caddy was in Daddy's driveway when I got there. My father and two salesmen leaned against it, waiting, their arms crossed.

"Write the check," my father commanded. "You're my executor."

"Should I tip them for delivery?"

Daddy shot me a look that conveyed meaning more concisely and more clearly than any words he might have formed, which would have been something like, *Don't be an idiot, Junior Joe-Boy.*

In the next nine months, that maroon Cadillac transported my parents to dozens of doctor appointments, chemotherapy infusions, and radiation treatments. It was not just a car, but a luxury car with leather seats and a smooth ride, and it became a sort of sanctuary for my father and me. We could say things on those comfortable seats that did not get repeated elsewhere.

To my surprise, on the way to meet his oncologist to discuss chemo, my father off-handedly gave me the same, detailed birds-and-bees summary he'd delivered to me when I was twelve. He was seventy-seven. I was forty-one, married, with two children. I did not protest.

He told me about when he and Hazel moved back to Florence and the *Morning News* published an article about his return. After describing the medical backgrounds of my mother and father, the reporter asked her how they met.

"'Well,' your mother said, 'we met in the operating room.' Then she said, 'We often scrubbed together.'"

We laughed, and I countered with the story of my first attempt to explore the wonders of the female breast. "It was a cold Saturday night. My date and I were at the drive-in. I leaned toward her and went to slip my hand down the top of her dress and was inches from glory when my hand could move no more. I'd shut the car door on the tail of my coat." Daddy thought that was funny.

During a chemo treatment, while my father was being hooked up to the IV, I received a call that my mother was having trouble breathing. I jumped up to leave, and my father moved to get up. The nurse and I quickly held him back.

"No, Daddy. You stay. I'll handle it."

My father wept. I had never seen him cry, never seen him shed a tear. I hugged him, and he buried his face in my chest and sobbed.

Inevitably, our trips became more frequent. If not chemo, my father needed x-rays or blood tests or his medication adjusted. One morning when I went by the house, my father wasn't there. Mama said he was at the office.

"At the *office*? How did he get there?"

He had called Marilyn, his office nurse of twenty years.

I rushed over and found my father sitting behind his desk, neatly dressed in a dark coat and tie.

"Daddy? What are you doing?" He didn't move.

It was like I wasn't there. He rose slowly and walked around his office, looking at books and family photos. He took his white coat from a hook on the back of the door. His hand gently traced his name embroidered on the front pocket.

"I'll never wear this coat again," he said.

I didn't know what to say. I moved behind him and put my arm around his shoulders.

"Give me the keys," he said. Though his eyes were cloudy, his stare was steely and serious: "Give them to me." I placed the keys in his open palm, and he led the way to the Cadillac. He slipped in behind the steering wheel, slid the key into the ignition and turned it. The car rumbled to life. He revved the engine a few times and smiled with satisfaction at the powerful sound. From his front pocket, he pulled out a cigar, ran it under his nose and breathed in the fragrance appreciatively. He lit it slowly, deliberately, following the rules for proper cigar lighting. As he exhaled a thin cloud of blue smoke, he smacked his lips with satisfaction.

On the way home, Daddy took his time, driving up and down the familiar streets of the neighborhood for a few minutes before letting the Caddy slow to a stop. He put the transmission into park, drew faintly on the stogie and pushed out a wisp of blue smoke. He looked at me with a gratified gleam in his dimmed eyes.

"Joe," he said, "there's really nothing that says 'life is fine' quite like a Cadillac and a good cigar."

Months passed. My father endured thirty radiation treatments and a final round of chemotherapy. One day I pulled the Cadillac into a parking space at the hospital, and before I could climb out, he took me gently by the arm.

"I regret that I was gone so much when y'all were young," he whispered.

The comment caught me off guard. I squeezed his hand.

"We understood, Daddy. You were busy, being on call, delivering babies. The phone rang, and you had to drop everything and rush to the hospital – in a *Pontiac*."

He laughed.

"But you were there at the first high school ball game I pitched. I didn't see you behind the fence until the last inning."

"I got there in the first inning. I was afraid I'd make you nervous, so I hid in the crowd."

"I didn't know that."

"I know," he said and shrugged. "You pitched well. A two-hitter."

My father's "proper procedure" for dressing was a coat and tie. Once while attending a medical convention with my mother, the fire alarm in their hotel sounded in the wee hours of the night, sending everyone outdoors in their pajamas and robes. Everyone, that is, except Daddy. When he and my mother reached the sidewalk, he was in coat, tie and wingtips. So it was strange, unsettling even, when his illness consigned him to a wheelchair, and he opted for an old gray jogging suit, covering his head with a brown wool cap. He also quit shaving.

On the way to one of his last radiation treatments, he dug around in the seat cushions, looking for his flip-up sunshades. Instead, he found a pair of my wife's baby-blue cat-eye sunglasses. He removed his glasses and put on hers.

"How do I look?"

"Like a homeless drag queen after a big night."

He laughed and kept the glasses on.

After eight months, there were no more treatments. All options were exhausted. So was he. I dropped by the house every day, and my father always asked if we had anywhere to go. I reminded him we didn't, that we had no more appointments.

One day he looked up at me from his wheelchair.

"Could we just ride around for a while?"

"Sure, Daddy."

"I miss our rides."

"Me too."

We took to the back roads, the country roads and wound up in Timmonsville, his old hometown. His eyesight was weak, so I called out the landmarks as we passed. As I did, he told me stories about his childhood: roller skating down the bumpy sidewalks, working in his father's grocery store during the Depression, joining the army in World War II, being informed by his father that, like it or not, he *would* go to medical school, his eventual choice of obstetrics because it was, he said, a happy specialty.

On the way home, I mustered the nerve to bring up a subject we'd managed to avoid on all those trips in the maroon Cadillac. The funeral. His funeral.

"What do you want to talk about," Daddy said.

"You know, the service," I said. "What hymns you want, that stuff."

He stared out the window for a moment.

"'He Leadeth Me,'" he said. "It was my mother's favorite."

This surprised me. He never talked much about his mother.

"And mahogany."

"Mahogany?"

"I want a mahogany casket."

Again I was surprised.

"You're sure? It'll be expensive."

"Dammit!" He slammed his fist on the padded dashboard, and I jumped. "I said I want a mahogany casket! You dicker with Charlie, dicker good. He's cheap, but you can wear him down. Take your time. The markup on those things is unbelievable, and you tell Charlie I know that." Daddy loved to dicker.

"Mahogany it is, then. What about pallbearers? I think we should ask Sonny."

"Sonny is a pallbearer at every funeral I've ever attended. Don't you think we're overusing him?"

"Not at all. You're one of his favorite relatives."

"He hasn't dropped anybody has he?" Daddy said.

"Not that I know of."

"Okay, call Sonny."

After my father died, I drove the Caddy to the mausoleum nearly every day for a while. I missed our talks more than I'd expected. The driving gave substance to my memories, so did visiting him, and so did his maroon Cadillac, and a good cigar. On the way home, I lit one.

He was right, you know. Life was fine.

# 17

## *The Revival*

I had always wanted to lead a revival, so I was overjoyed when the pastor of Mount Hebron Baptist Church issued an invitation to do just that. As a hospital chaplain, I was considered by some not to be a *real* preacher. I welcomed the chance to help them reconsider.

In the Southern Baptist tradition, revivals are somewhat odd affairs. Over the course of four nights, I was expected to deliver searing sermons of rebuke to the members of Mount Hebron, who were lowly sinners in peril of eternal flames and the horrors of hell unless they repented. In return for supplying these scathing threats, I was to be paid an honorarium and, each night, dine on fried chicken, rice and gravy, casseroles, biscuits and apple pie with a family from the congregation.

The success of any revival, and the effectiveness of the evangelist, is measured by the number of souls who come forward to declare their repentance. Therein lay my problem.

I found that leading a revival was not the simple yet awe-inspiring event I'd hoped it would be. Despite three nights of strenuously trying to instill fear, guilt and shame, not a single chastised soul came forward. A few could have faked it and walked down the aisle out of plain Christian charity, but none did. Three times at bat with no hits, but I was undeterred. I was warmed up. Surely the reliable *Moses Gets a Church*, my strongest sermon, would rattle the scruples of a few members and pull them from the comfort of their pews.

My scripture for that last evening was from Exodus 18:13-27, which tells the story of an encounter between Moses and his father-in-law Jethro, who watched Moses act as judge in the disputes of his people. From my place behind the pulpit, I slowly scanned the congregation and allowed a silence to fall over the crowd.

"Imagine," I began. "Moses sits comfortably in his lawn chair, shaded from the hot sun by the canopy of his tent. Before him passes a line of sweaty, disgruntled Israelites pouring out their woes for Moses to settle. One young man, like the others, stands in line for hours in the desert heat and sun, waiting his turn to speak to Moses. His turn finally comes, and he states his case. Moses eyes this parishioner, points a stern finger in his face and unleashes a scorching diatribe against the man. Dejected, the young Israelite dutifully pays Moses homage and walks away, resigned but unsatisfied. From his seat in the far corner of the tent, Jethro watches and strokes his long beard. Jethro wasn't just Moses' father-in-law; he was also a priest of Midian and, at 120, was a seasoned veteran of the ministry. Moses, only in his eighties, was still considered a novice."

I decided on the fly to inject a bit of humor.

"By the way, I have a bit of trivia that might interest you. Jethro Bodine, of the famed *Beverly Hillbillies,* is a known descendent of Jethro the priest. I researched this myself."

It fell flat, but I could do better. I hurried on to describe a mid-morning break in which Moses and Jethro have a conversation.

"Moses puts a couple of shekels in the drink machine and buys Jethro and himself a Coke.

"'So how about these crazy Israelites and their silly domestic problems?' Moses quips, as he hands a Coke to his father-in-law. In return, Jethro offers the raw rookie a few well-chosen words of wisdom.

"'Moses, my son, what in Sheol are you doing? Why do you sit comfortable and at ease while your people suffer all day in the sun and wilt in the heat waiting to speak to you?'

"Moses chokes on his Coke. He thought Jethro was pleased with his efforts.

"'What in the world do you mean?' he replies. 'I settle the people's disputes and make sure they know God's statutes.'

"Frustrated, Jethro says, 'Moses, Moses, my young dimwit of a son-in-law. Just take a look at all those miserable people. They stand for long hours in the heat, no sunscreen, nothing to drink. This is not good. Not good at all. Look, they already murmur.' By that, he meant they were getting fed up. 'You're not only wearing them out, Moses, but yourself as well. You attempt too much. This is becoming too heavy a thing for you.'"

From my perch in the pulpit, I sensed I had them in the palm of my hand. Energized, I let the spirit flow into me and continued.

"Jethro then explains God's will for Moses.

"'Delegate!' he says. 'To carry out God's will, you must learn to delegate these tasks. You must choose able men to help you. This will quench the murmuring, and then you won't need those pills. What do you call them?'

"'Valium,' says Moses.

"'Yes. You won't have to take any more of that to settle your nerves.'

"Well now, Moses heeds the words of Jethro. He chooses groups of men qualified to handle the routine matters, while he reserves his authority to deal with the more difficult cases. And it works. Moses preserves his strength, gets off the meds and the murmuring stops. He goes on to a stellar forty-year career wandering in the desert before finally leading his people to the Promised Land."

I paused for effect, gripped the pulpit and leaned forward. My voice grew stronger, and I zeroed in on my prey.

"Is *your* life overloaded? Are *you* on medication because your load has become too heavy? Do *you* try to face life's demands all by yourself? Is there *murmuring* in your camp?"

Now they were all set for the climax.

"*Jesus*," I cried, my voice even stronger. "*Jesus* is the answer! In Matthew 11:28-30, he says, 'Come unto me all ye who labor and are heavy-laden, and I will give you rest. Take my yoke upon you, and learn of me; for I am meek and lowly in heart: and ye shall find rest unto your souls. For my yoke is easy, and my burden is light.'"

Like all good TV evangelists, I took out my handkerchief and wiped the sweat from my brow.

"So come to Jesus. Unload the burdens of your life.

He will give you rest! In Jesus there is no more murmuring. Jesus will help you delegate the tasks that wear you out. Come to Jesus and find peace!"

Pretty good stuff, I thought. Then I put a tidy bow on my eloquence: I hit them with a quote from R. W. Evans's 1842 *The Bishopric of Souls:*

"'For it is the trick of the devil by which he deceives good souls, to entice them to do more than they can, so that they may be unable to do anything at all. The Spirit of God on the contrary, entices one gently to do good as reasonably as one can, so that one may do it perseveringly for a long time.'"

Wham. Case closed. We shared an impassioned prayer and then sang fifty verses of "Just As I Am" while I waited for the contrite souls to stream down the aisle.

None came. Not one.

I couldn't believe it. I had failed. Where did I go wrong? All the fixings were there – a strong message, strongly delivered, tempered with plenty of humor. But it fell flat. Maybe if they gave me just one more night . . . I'd do it for free.

There's a funny thing about sermons. They are sometimes merely projections of the preacher's mind. I didn't want to quit. I *knew* I could make them repent. I *had* to make them repent. My entire reputation as a preacher depended on it! Who wants an evangelist who can't save souls? These were my projections, but they went further. The sermon was about my own personal, private struggle. The fact was that, like Moses and many others, mine was an overburdened life.

Beyond a shadow of a doubt, God called me to be the chaplain at McLeod Regional Medical Center. I was needed there, like Moses was needed in the desert. Every day I walked the floors of the hospital visiting all the units – Oncology, Surgical Intensive Care, Cardiac Intensive Care, the Emergency Room. If a patient needed to see a chaplain at noon or the middle of the night, I was there. If there was a death, I comforted the family. If there was an over-stressed nurse, I was a sympathetic counselor.

I had a great group of pastors who volunteered several days a week as chaplains. They all were willing and able to help, but I didn't make good use of them. I tried "to perform it alone," as Jethro told Moses.

I also faced the daily demands of my young family. My wife worked as a nurse on the afternoon shift. Before work each day, she took care of the house and Mac and Blakely, who were five and two at the time. In the evening after work, I relieved the babysitter, fed and bathed the kids and got them to bed. If Nancy and I saw each other for any length of time, it was usually at the hospital.

In the middle of this hectic life, I had decided to pursue my Doctor of Ministry degree, in part because I'd failed to become a medical doctor like my father. To ensure that my generation had a Doctor Baroody, I was determined to earn my doctorate. My research project involved, ironically, helping cancer nurses cope with the pressures of caring for patients with terminal illnesses.

So on top of all that, why accept the invitation to chastise the pitiful souls at Mount Hebron? I was already encumbered, why take on more? Well, I had always wanted to lead a revival, and it was only for that one week. We needed the money. What could it hurt?

On the day of my final sermon, I had an early morning meeting at the hospital, and then had to be eighty miles away in Columbia three hours later for a consultation on my doctoral project. Before leaving the hospital, I made a few pastoral visits and talked with the minister covering for me. When I got back from Columbia that afternoon, I made a few more visits and then rushed home. I paid the babysitter, changed into my preacher suit, crammed the kids into the car with all their paraphernalia and took off for my mother-in-law's house twenty miles away.

I was running behind, of course. I said a quick hello, threw the kids and their stuff out of the car and sped away. Ten miles and fifteen minutes later, I sat at the dinner table with the night's host family, wolfing down fried chicken and biscuits, confident that this, *this* was the night. I walked into the church at 8 p.m., delivered the golden words and got zilch for my efforts. Dejected, I slinked back to my mother-in-law's, retrieved the kids and was headed home by 10:05.

I was barely out of the driveway when Blakely, strapped in her car seat, began crying. With one hand on the wheel, I used the other to reach into the back seat and pat her on the leg. That didn't soothe her, so I pulled into a gas station, gave her diaper a quick finger-check. It came back clear, so I stuck her pacifier in her mouth, and she spit it back at me. I searched the diaper bag and found a box of animal crackers and ate a handful. I gave the rest to her, and she settled down.

Beside me in the front seat, Mac was looking out the window at the night sky. As I started driving again, he fired off a rapid string of questions.

"How many stars are there? Where does the sun go at night? Is there *really* a man in the moon? Why does he follow us around?" Before I could poke a word in edgewise, he was on to the next question.

Half-chewed animal crackers peppered me in the back of the head, and Blakely started crying again. I drove while blindly searching for the pacifier. Mac's questions pounded in my ears. A car honked and swerved when I veered into the oncoming lane. I got back on my side of the road and told Mac to find Blakely's sippy cup. He ignored me and kept up the questions. I pulled off the road again and jerked the car to a stop. I found the cup and gave it to her. It was only ten more miles to home. I told Mac I would give him five dollars if he would just shut up until we got there. The sippy cup flew onto the dashboard, and Blakely wailed.

"*Shut up!*" I shouted. "Will you both just shut up!"

I hit Mac, slapped him hard on the thigh.

"Do you hear me?" I yelled, and the questions stopped. He looked at the floor. I squeezed his jaw and jerked his face toward me. "Look at me when I'm talking to you!" He tried to pull away, and I squeezed harder. "Do not say another word!"

He was terrified and timidly crawled into the back seat. Blakely's wailing went on and on, and so did my yelling. Mac found his sister's pacifier, put it in her mouth, and hugged her, looking fearfully at the back of my head. I watched them in the rearview mirror, and my anger dissolved into shame and guilt.

With five miles to go, the silence was deafening. Another car honked, and I swerved again.

And then Jethro spoke in my ears.

"What you are doing is not good . . .," he said.

Then R. W. Evans whispered, "For it is the trick of the devil by which he deceives good souls. . . ."

I checked the rearview again. Mac and Blakely were sound asleep. They looked like little angels. A fresh wave of guilt washed over me.

I turned into our driveway, and Nancy's car wasn't there. It must be a long night for her, I thought. I walked Mac into the house with Blakely on my shoulder. After putting them to bed, I went back outside to unload the car. My failed sermon nagged at me.

"You attempt too much," Jethro whispered. "This is becoming too heavy a thing for you."

"So that you may be unable to do anything at all," Reverend Evans said.

They were right. I had been deceiving myself, letting myself surrender to the delusion that I could and must do it all alone.

I checked on Blakely, still sound asleep in her crib. I entered Mac's room, and he raised his head with fear still in his eyes, fear I had put there . . . fear of me.

My time to repent had come. I crossed the room and kneeled at Mac's bedside. I softly stroked his jaw and kissed his cheek. After a moment, he gave me a smile.

"There are 157.8 trillion billion stars in the sky,"

I said. "The sun sleeps all night while the man in the moon watches over us. He follows us because we need watching."

Mac hugged my neck, and I sat down on the bed and lay beside him.

I woke at the sound of the front door opening. I got up and, rubbing my eyes, found Nancy bent over and rummaging in the fridge. She looked up and smiled.

"So how was the revival?" she asked. "Anyone repent?"

"Just one."

"Good. That's better than none, right?"

# 18

## *Peacoat*

The men's room near my hospital office is hard for visitors to find. There is a big sign in the lobby reading "MEN" and pointing to my corridor, but once in the hallway, the man in need must find the bathroom on his own. Seeing no more signs, many start trying all the doors. The chapel is the first one they try. The chaplain's office, my office, is second. Both are clearly labeled. I get these fellows all the time. Sometimes they knock, but mostly they just open my door and blush when they see me. I tell them it's on their right, just past the short brick wall, and away they go.

I came around the corner one winter day and saw one of these gentlemen leaning on my office door, his head pressed against the wood. His suit was rumpled and ill-fitting on his slight frame. Sparse white hair poked out from his head at odd angles. I put him in his seventies. Most men in a hurry don't stand still like that. He clutched the doorknob. Maybe he was waiting for me.

I touched his shoulder.

"Sir? Mister? May I help you?"

He didn't respond. I pointed toward the brick wall.

"The men's room is right over there."

He still did not budge.

"See?" I said. "Look here. Right there. Just behind

that brick wall."

"No," he mumbled.

"Yes, it's there. You just can't see it from here."

"No," he repeated.

I stepped out into the corridor and, with a swoop of my arm, pointed the way.

The man did not move.

"You're looking for the bathroom, right?"

"Yep," the man said.

"You couldn't be any closer."

"Not close enough."

"Why?"

"Because, I done got started."

"Started? Started with what?"

"With, with . . . *going*."

"What? Well stop going! You've got to stop going!"

"I can't stop." Still looking down. Head against the door.

"Why not? Why can't you stop?"

"I told you. Because I *done* got started!"

I noticed a wet spot forming around the crotch of his pants. "But you've got to stop! That's my door you're standing in front of!"

A few seconds passed. Still looking downward, he said, "Okay. I think I stopped."

"Good. Let me help you to the men's room."

"Oh, no! If I try to move, I'll . . . I'll get started again."

I moved close behind him and placed my hands on his shoulders. He tensed up even more. "Look, let me help you. You can walk without getting started again. Just take a slow, deep breath and try to hold it."

He inhaled slowly, puffing out his cheeks.

"Don't hold your breath, hold your water. Breathe deep and relax and squeeze tight."

He took his hand off the door and clutched at his crotch. I guided him away from the door.

"Okay," I said. "We're on the way. Follow my lead."

He relaxed and nodded, and I saw his face for the first time. It was a nice face, under the anguish and shame. He did not meet my eyes.

Dancing an awkward waltz, one side step at a time, we made it without incident. Inside he unzipped, hugged a urinal and found relief.

I waited by the sink. When he was done, he flushed and washed his hands. For the first time, we stood face to face.

"I . . . I don't know what to say," he said. "Thank you. Thank you. You really saved me back there."

"That's my calling."

"Who are you?"

"I'm the hospital chaplain. That was my door you were leaning on."

"Oh. Sorry, Reverend." He looked down at the now rather large wet spot on his pants.

"You should probably go home," I said.

"Oh, I can't do that."

"Oh?"

"Not right now. I'm here with my wife. We're from out of town. Her sister had surgery. I'm stuck here all day."

I checked my watch. I was late for a meeting of the Ethics Committee.

"Well, you can't go out there looking like that."

The door opened, and a young red-headed kid, maybe three or four, walked in ahead of a man with the same color hair. The boy pointed at the old man's pants.

"Look, Daddy, he made a boo-boo." His father smiled sheepishly and hustled him into a stall.

Feeling rushed, I wracked my brain, trying to come up with something to do. The trouble with wracking is knowing when to stop. Maybe I stopped too soon.

"Wait here. I've got a coat you can use." I had worn my new London Fog peacoat that day. My wife had given it to me for Christmas. I rushed back to my office and returned with the coat, passing the carrot-topped duo on their way out.

"Here you go." I held out the coat.

"You shouldn't do this. I'll be fine," the man protested. "I can wash it out."

"It's okay. Don't worry." I helped him into the coat. "Drop it off with the ladies at the information desk on your way out. I'll pick it up later."

The coat was way too big, but it did the job. I could get it cleaned tomorrow.

"Look, I've got to run. Good luck to you."

"Thank you, sir. I appreciate your help. Sorry for, uh, messing up your day. I'll leave your coat at the desk."

Riding the elevator to my meeting, I thought about that saying of Jesus, or was it John the Baptist? I couldn't quite place it, but it was the one about sharing your coat with someone in need. A warm glow of self-satisfaction came over me. Not only had I loaned this guy a coat, it was my new London Fog. That was *really* going the extra mile. Jesus was patting the empty seat at his right hand and looking at me.

Later that day I checked at the information desk in the lobby. The ladies told me no coat had been returned, London Fog or otherwise. At the close of the day, it was the same story. Had the old man suckered me? I had never gotten his name or the room number of his sister-in-law. I hadn't even thought about it.

I told Nancy about it when I got home. She wasn't nearly as impressed with my good deed as I had been.

"The London Fog? Oh, Joe, why didn't you just get him some scrubs? You've seen the last of that coat." She didn't call me foolish, but I could see she was thinking it.

The wintery cold and drizzle continued the next morning. My green hooded slicker, the one I call Kermit, took the place of the missing London Fog. I'd had it for years. It was an old friend, and it felt right. Nancy says I'm the only person she knows who has personal relationships with his clothes. I was hoping to have one with Mr. London Fog.

I unlocked my office door and noticed another needful fellow doing the potty dance outside the chapel.

"Men's room?" I called. He nodded urgently, and I pointed the way. Maybe I ought to have a new sign placed on the chapel door, I thought. One that says:

*This is my room. To find your room,*
*look behind you, past the brick wall.*
*Pray here. Pee there.*
 *God*

I started my rounds in the Emergency Room, where things were slow. I chatted with one of the nurses, an old friend who completely agreed with Nancy about the coat. But I still had hope. I passed the security desk on my way to the floors. In a wheelchair nearby, a young man with a bandaged leg adjusted a blanket to cover his injury. Crutches lay across the armrests. Behind the desk, a nursing assistant was pulling a coat, a London Fog, off the coat rack. She threw it around her shoulders, carefully pulled the blanket up to the injured man's neck, and pushed him outside into the chilly drizzle.

I was convinced it was mine but wasn't close enough to be certain. Outside, a family member held up the coat to keep the patient and his helper dry while the awkward transition from wheelchair to car was made. A large portico provided some shelter, but the coat stopped the cold breeze and wet mist from blowing through. My beeper went off, calling me to an emergency at the critical care unit before I could examine the coat.

An hour later I was back, but the coat wasn't. The security guard remembered it from my description but didn't know what had become of it.

"That coat sure has seen a lot of use," the guard said, nodding at the cold raw day outside. "I'll page you if it shows up, Dr. Baroody."

No page came. Subsequent checks at the information desk returned the same result. If the coat in the ER had indeed been my London Fog, the old man must have used that exit and dropped it off on his way out. With all the hands it passed through, somebody had decided to keep it. Oh, well. I had hardly gotten to know Mr. Fog. My consolation was that my new friend had met and comforted more than a few people in the past few days. And I still had my old green friend, Kermit.

As it turns out, John the Baptist – that crotchety, desert-dwelling, locust-eating, doomsday-preacher – spoke the words about the coat. I found the passage in Luke 3:11. He had denounced the crowd waiting to be dunked in the River Jordan as a brood of vipers. They were deceiving themselves if they believed baptism or being a descendant of Abraham would save them from their sinful ways. The people were afraid and asked John the Baptist what they should do. The Baptizer answered, "He who has two coats, let him share one with him who has none. . . ."

The coat to which John referred was actually a tunic, a nonessential inner garment often worn by travelers. But what he meant was true all the same. Don't keep more than is necessary, he was saying, share your non-essentials with those in need.

While I did not expect my new peacoat to become a "peecoat," it did and I'm okay with that.

# 19

## *The Next Will Clark*

From childhood to his late teens, baseball was my son Mac's ticket. His dream – my dream for him – was to play in the major leagues. Of course most boys playing little league held that dream but, as it turned out, Mac had a real shot.

You wouldn't think so at first. Once, when he was three, we were playing on a see-saw. I came down too hard on my end and sent Mac into orbit. As he soared through the air over my right shoulder, I tried to snare him, but I missed. He belly-flopped hard onto the sandy part of the playground and then lay motionless. I thought for sure he was dead. In the two beats it took me to free myself and come to his side, Mac let loose with a belly laugh the likes of which I had never heard.

Mac was the youngest and usually the smallest kid on the baseball team. Like any good father, I encouraged him (some would say coached him) from the sidelines.

"Let's go, Mac. Give it to him. Show him what you've got!" I covertly flashed my index finger, the signal for a fastball, as if Mac (at eleven years old) had one or any other pitch for that matter.

The batter he faced was six feet tall and needed a shave. Mac took a handkerchief from his back pocket.

He was not sweating. I knew this trick. His motions were clean and deliberate. He finished unfolding the cloth and blotted his forehead, then returned it to his back pocket. Mac was in control, sizing up the batter, trying to throw off the player's timing. When Mac wound up and hurled the pitch, there was a solid *whack* and his fastball went soaring over the centerfielder's head. As he should, Mac raced over to back up the third baseman, but the throw went to home plate instead. He had to cover home, and the big guy was charging down the third base line. I shut my eyes. Mac was gonna get creamed.

Through one peeking eye, I saw the throw didn't make it. Rather than flattening Mac, the big kid just picked him up, threw him over his shoulder and carried him across home plate. Everyone – both sides – cheered.

Growing up, I also played baseball. At one time, there was talk I might get drafted by the pros. As a left-handed high school pitcher, my fastball was unhittable. The problem was I also had a hard time getting it over the plate. In one game, I struck out 15 batters, but I also walked nine, most of them in one horrendous inning.

By the time Mac reached high school, he was almost six feet tall. A weightlifting program bulked him up and improved his speed. Mac had become a slick-fielding shortstop with a terrific arm, and he showed good promise as a hitter. During his senior year, college and pro scouts began to notice. Their interest took off at the prestigious Georgetown Invitational Tournament.

South Florence High School, ranked in the state's top ten, was invited to play.

A steady rain fell during their first game against Stratford, the number one team. I pulled the hood of my green slicker, Mr. Kermit, over my head as Mac strode to the plate. With a runner on second, the pitcher's ninety-mile-per-hour fastball whizzed through the rain, popped into the catcher's mitt and the umpire called strike one.

I tensed up, clapped, whistled and hollered encouragement from my place behind the fence. I could hear Nancy calling Mac's name. The next moment was like a scene from the movie *The Natural*, where aging player Roy Hobbs (Robert Redford) hits a ball that flies up and shatters the stadium lights in centerfield. Mac pounded the ball hard, and it soared high and far through the glistening rain, landing in the top row of the centerfield bleachers, 403 feet away.

Two innings later he did it again.

I was ecstatic. With each home run, I ran with Mac as he trotted down the third-base line. It was as if *I* hit both of those home runs.

I've always thought of myself as a supportive parent. The idea of being "overinvolved" never occurred to me, but the game against West Florence for the unofficial city championship really should have given me a clue.

That morning I went to the rector of St. John's Episcopal Church and asked if he had any holy water. The rector removed a vial of water taken from the River Jordan. *Can't get much better than that.* With that vial and the *Book of Common Prayer*, I snuck onto the West

Florence baseball field around noon and ran to the shortstop position.

Sprinkling the water between second and third where Mac would play, I read out loud from the prayer book (It didn't count unless you prayed out loud.): "Oh Lord, our heavenly Father, we beseech thee to bless my son Mac, who will play here tonight. May he do great things. May the other team suck." (I did a little adlibbing.)

I barely outran the security officers who had received a report of a deranged man chanting on the ball diamond. I got away but, sadly, South Florence lost the game.

Nancy and I were proud and delighted on the day Mac signed to play college ball at the University of South Carolina. The photographer told me I needed to stand behind Mac, not hang over him, when he signed the letter of intent. Nancy kicked me in the shin to emphasize the point.

Mac did well his freshman year at USC, starting several games at second base, and was also a pinch-runner, a pinch-hitter and a late-inning replacement. The schedule was grueling. The USC team played sixty games and practiced on the off-days. Post-season, Mac played another sixty games in a summer collegiate league.

During Christmas break of his sophomore season, Mac came into my bedroom holding his garnet-and-black jacket. Pinned to the USC letters across the front was a tiny gold baseball.

"Wow," I said. "Mind if I try it on?"

I admired myself in the mirror as I closed the snaps

on the front of the jacket. Mac stood off to the side. I snapped open the jacket and handed it back to him, but Mac said, "You keep it, Dad. It's what you always wanted." I protested. It was his, I said. He had earned it. But Mac declined to take it back and quietly left the room.

Later that January, Mac called us from school. The team was practicing in preparation for the season opener in February. Mac had earned the starting spot at second base. His tone was somber. "I'm not sure I want to play anymore. My heart's just not in it like it used to be." He reminded us of how much fun he'd had surfing in Fiji. Next to baseball, surfing was his passion. I was shocked! How could he give up his dream? His coaches had told him he stood a good chance of being drafted in the top ten rounds! I pleaded with him to reconsider. He finally agreed to give it more time.

Two weeks later we drove to Columbia for a game. Mac told us that, if he decided to quit, he would be waiting for us in the parking lot. If not, he would be on the field. I recalled the time his mother and I took Mac and his friends to Atlanta to see the Braves play the San Francisco Giants. Mac was one of the chosen few who got an autograph from Giants' superstar Will "The Thrill" Clark. On the way home, Mac was so excited he spilled his chocolate milkshake while boasting to his friends that he would be the next Will Clark. I looked at Nancy. She looked at me. We grinned.

I pulled the car into the stadium parking lot, found a space and parked. Nancy and I got out. She put out her hand at the same moment I put out mine. We linked fingers and anxiously followed the rowdy crowd toward the stadium. We stepped onto the sidewalk, jostled by fans filtering in before and behind us. I tried not to but couldn't help scanning the parking lot, my eyes darting left and right, looking but hoping not to see Mac. I could see that Nancy was doing the same thing. We passed under the canopy of a large live oak. Next to the trunk of the massive tree, Mac stood stock-still waiting for us.

"Well, I did it," Mac said.

My heart sank.

"I quit," he said.

I didn't know what to say.

I looked at him. I was visibly upset.

Nancy squeezed my hand hard, reminding me to think before I spoke.

I asked Mac how he felt. He let loose with a belly laugh I had only heard once before.

"I feel like I've been let out of jail," he said.

We got lunch and headed home. Mac talked nonstop about his plans. "I'm thinking about the seminary. . . . I'm thinking about the military. . . . I think I'd like to get married."

"But you're not even dating anyone," Nancy said.

Mac adjusted himself in his seat as he considered his mother's comment. "This is only a minor hurdle," he said. "Heck, the pursuit will be great fun." In moving about, Mac managed to knock the Coke in his hand and it spilled on the car floor. He pulled out a handkerchief from his back pocket, carefully unfolding the cloth. He blotted the carpet, then neatly refolded the handkerchief.

With tears in my eyes, I watched it all through the rearview mirror.

"I don't know what I'm going to do next," Mac said. "But I know somehow I'm going to be me – the next Mac Baroody." He looked in the rearview mirror. I caught the smile on his face, and he caught mine.

# 20

## *My Daughter's Wedding*

Five minutes before the wedding began, I was where I'd been for most of the afternoon, in a vestibule in the church, waiting. Three hours of twiddling my thumbs. I blamed it on the wedding director. She said there were pictures to be taken, but few had involved me. I was there because my daughter was getting married, and I had nowhere else to go and no idea what to do with myself.

Blakely swept into the vestibule, serene in her white off-the-shoulder, beaded wedding gown. Her veil flowed gracefully down her back like angel's wings. With her bouquet in one hand, she kneeled beside the young son of a friend and tickled his chin. The little boy laughed and gave her a big smile.

From my place by the door, I thought back to the fear Nancy and I felt that day twenty-three years ago when the pediatrician told us Blakely's heart had a hole in it – a condition known as ventricular septal defect – and that it might require surgery. Thankfully that proved unnecessary, but it was a looming dread, never far from our thoughts.

The little boy darted away, and Blakely rose, saw me and smiled. Three minutes to go. I craned my neck for a peek inside. The wedding party was in place. My jitters returned.

"Hurry up!" I said under my breath. "Get over here! It's time!" Blakely giggled. She actually seemed to be enjoying herself. In measured strides, she floated to my side, kissed my cheek and took my arm. I squeezed her tight against me.

The wedding chimes sounded.

For a moment, the sound, or more specifically what the sound meant, failed to register. Perhaps it was the abject terror in my eyes, or the death grip with which I hugged her arm to me, but somehow my daughter sensed my desperation.

"It's okay, Daddy," she whispered softly. "If you ease up on my arm, we'll be able to breathe better." I did, and she was right.

"So we start walking when the chimes stop," I said.

"Yes, we do." She smiled proudly at me. "You look nice."

The chimes stopped. The doors to the sanctuary opened. The wedding director nudged us forward as 400 people thundered to their feet and turned their 800 eyes toward us.

Blakely tugged on my arm, and we started walking. Almost immediately she tugged on my arm again, this time to slow me down.

"It's supposed to be a walk, Daddy, not a run," she whispered out of the corner of her mouth. I could see her point.

Up at the altar, Blakely's older brother, was grinning down on us. Mac was in seminary, and the plan was for him to begin the ceremony, and, after giving Blakely away, I would take my place beside my son and continue the service. At the time we hatched it, it seemed like a good plan. I was not so sure now.

We arrived at the front of the church. The congregants found their seats again, and my son began the ceremony.

"Today we gather here among family and friends, and before God, to join Blakely and Buddy together in holy matrimony."

My knees went shaky and weak. This was actually happening. I wasn't going to wake up from this dream with my daughter still twelve. Oddly, it wasn't the bride's finery or the decking of the halls that drove that point home. It was Mac, standing there all grown-up and mature and composed, instructing us about God and marriage. *Holy Jesus! This was real.*

I felt myself swaying.

I thought about those nights when Blakely was a baby, when I put her across my shoulder, patted her back and rocked back and forth on my feet while she learned to fall asleep.

I saw Blakely when she was four, rushing at me in my recliner, squealing that Mac was torturing her and demanding to know what I was going to do about it. I picked her up and plopped her in my lap, kissed her forehead, and told her to please go ask Mama to get my gun so I could shoot Mac and end her misery. This plan of action seemed to please her.

Regularly at that age, Blakely would come to our room in the middle of the night and crawl in between Nancy and me. As the "man of the house" I had to show Blakely that I was in charge, so I would carry her back to her bed and admonish her to stay in her own room. A few minutes later, I would feel her crawling back in our bed. This process was repeated until, in the interest of my own sanity, I finally relented and traded beds with her. The routine evolved into her tapping me on the shoulder, and giving me the signal with her thumb to leave.

I remembered walking her down the aisles of dark theaters. We battled over who would hold the popcorn. I claimed proper movie-going procedure required that I guard the popcorn to ensure that not a single kernel passed our lips until the previews were over and the movie itself actually started, a practice she upholds to this day.

Then there was that time her kindergarten teacher sent a note home with her. I asked my wife why in the world Blakely got a note from the teacher. Nancy told me she didn't get the note; I did. Her teacher wanted me to quit walking her to the classroom, hanging up her coat, seeing her to her desk, and hugging and kissing her goodbye. She said I had to let my daughter out at the front entrance like the other parents.

The memories kept coming, strangely vivid recollections: I was there running, not walking, behind Blakely, steadying the bicycle while she completed her ritual of getting her hair just so and her clothes arranged just right.

Then, suddenly, I saw her at twelve when I took her and some friends to the Myrtle Beach Pavilion. I had to maintain a twenty-five-foot buffer behind her because being seen in public with your father was utterly unthinkable.

I remembered when Buddy called on me at my office back in October. His visit, and its purpose, was not a mystery. I asked him what was on his mind, then sat quietly and waited for him to speak. He didn't hesitate. In an easy, even tone, he got right to the point.

"I love your daughter," he said simply. "I love Blakely."

I let the moment linger, to make him squirm a little.

"You realize," I said gravely, "my daughter doesn't like anything that involves sweating." He knew that. I reminded him that she had enough clothes and shoes for a small country. He knew that, too. It did not matter. He loved her.

"She takes long showers and dries her hair with a blow dryer that dims lights all over town." He noted this but said it would not be a problem. There was only one place left for me to go.

"I can see you are a serious man. I will speak to you seriously. Do not, if you value your life and your sanity, do not ever go shopping for Blakely. Ever. Even if she gives you a detailed list, do not go. Trust me, I know. I've been through this with her mother. You will never bring the right thing home. One of the top ten reasons for repenting of your sins is that, if you don't, you are likely to spend eternity in hell shopping for your wife and always bringing home the wrong item."

He was undaunted.

"I love your daughter," he said. "I want to marry her."

I let that sink in for a moment, then offered my hand.

His firm and unwavering insistence impressed me. What mattered most to him was that he loved Blakely and that she loved him. Marriage was the natural result of their love, he said, their next step. I liked that a lot.

Mac's voice pulled me from my reverie and back to the wedding.

"Who gives Blakely to be married to Buddy?" Apparently, it was the second time he'd asked the question. I guess I missed it the first time. So the moment had arrived. The question hung in the air, awaiting my reply. I had posed this simple question to many brides' fathers over the years. It was no big deal. Not then. But this was different. *This* was a big deal. This was *my* daughter that *my* son was asking me about. I'm pretty sure not everyone understood just how *huge* this was. How did I fail to see this coming? Adrift in time and memory, I kept seeing things I had forgotten, slumbering memories that were suddenly waking up. Did this happen to *everyone?*

Suddenly, there I was with Mac and Blakely at Magnolia Mall, rushing toward Carolina Baby, where Mac said Mama took them if they needed to potty. Mac had urgently expressed his need. He was six. Blakely was two and still needed a stroller. We burst into the store, and I looked around quickly. I spotted a curtained doorway and, leaving Blakely in the stroller, I pushed aside the curtain and found a door marked "Restroom." I shoved Mac in and closed the door, then plopped down on the floor and heaved a sigh of relief. Two women screamed, babies began to wail and I think I wet my pants.

"You pervert!" one bellowed.

"Get out! Right *now!*" the other one agreed.

They were two very irate breastfeeding women, one with a twin latched onto each breast. I scrambled to my feet and fled out into the store. I found Blakely diaper-deep in more mayhem. Free from the stroller, she had cleared two shelves of baby clothes, another of books, including one touting the benefits of breastfeeding. I haphazardly restocked the shelves and was putting Blakely back in the stroller when Mac returned. He looked up at me scornfully.

"I can't leave you two alone for a second," he said in a fair imitation of his mother's favorite phrase.

Now here Mac was, all grown up and instructing Blakely and me again.

Mac's words came filtered by distance. My mind went back to the October night I took them, eleven and eight at the time, to the Eastern Carolina Agricultural Fair. Mac and Blakely conspired to con me into taking them, even though I hated the fair. Sticky cotton candy and rides that went in circles at ungodly speeds, these did not set well with me or my digestion. But we went anyway.

"This is a slow roller coaster," Mac claimed. We crammed ourselves into one of the rickety cars and began a slow, circular course. Not bad, I thought. Then it sped up. Faster and faster we went, and my heart kept pace. They had done it again. My children had tricked me again. Faster and faster we went, bouncing over little bumps, swinging around curves. Cotton candy slapped me in the face. Mac pointed at me and laughed. The roller coaster stopped. Relieved, I fought to free myself from the car and was thrown back into my seat as we took off again, flying backwards down the tracks. The hotdog I just ate was desperate for daylight and was debating which door to take. I held my breath and prayed, and apparently one of them worked because soon it was over.

I was alone in the flimsy car. Mac and Blakely had rushed off. Eyes open or eyes closed, everything spun wildly around. I stumbled to level ground and collapsed. Smelly sawdust stuck to my face and hair. A mostly eaten candy apple touched my lips. But the world had stopped whirling and I was glad for the stillness. So was my stomach.

"Mac," Blakely said happily. "Let's ride the Tilt-A-Whirl while Daddy takes a nap."

And off they went.

Mac was talking again.

"Who gives Blakely to be married to Buddy," Mac asked for the third time. Blakely elbowed me in the ribs. I coughed and said "ouch," suddenly coming to my senses.

"Her mother and I do," I said loud enough for all 800 ears to hear. Inside my head, the words echoed back and forth.

I awkwardly placed Blakely's hand in Buddy's and kissed her cheek through her veil, then made my way to Mac's side. With a booming voice, Mac said to the gathering, "Marriage is a celebration of the transcendent mystery of the couple's love and faithfulness." *What did he know of marriage*, I thought loudly to myself. Then, as rehearsed, Mac handed off the ceremony to me.

From the start of all this wedding stuff, I had been firm about wanting to both walk Blakely down the aisle *and* perform the ceremony. My wife bluntly questioned my sanity, not a new idea for her. Her only stipulations were that I "not act silly" and "not say anything stupid." Always solid advice.

I looked past Blakely's and Buddy's expectant faces to the larger sea of faces fixed on me, gravely waiting for my words to flow forth. I was waiting, too.

As usual, Nancy was right. What the hell was I thinking? Only an idiot would think he could walk his daughter calmly down the aisle, hand her off to some guy and then conduct the ceremony that forged them together as husband and wife. Only an idiot would do something like that.

The congregation stared at me. My eyes darted around the room. I was numb. I was stupid. I was mute. I saw the familiar, hopeful faces of relatives and friends. I saw Stewart, my cousin. We grew up together. Roomed together in college. Tried to pick up girls in off-campus bars a thousand times. He was enjoying my misery. He covertly shot me "the bird," winked and then held up an encouraging thumb.

My sermon was on the lectern in front of me, my homily, neatly typed in capital letters so I could read it easily. I picked it up. It was as though I had never seen it before. Everything about the wedding – the music, the gown, the menu, the cake, the flowers, the band for the reception – all that and much more had been decided with little input from me. Blakely and Nancy were much better at these things. But this homily, these words, *my* words, strung together by my pen – this was my contribution, my gift. But I did not recognize these words, and not only because the paper was shaking so hard. I looked to the crowd, then to the vibrating words. I had to say something . . . *something* . . . and then the words finally came to me, and I spoke. They were not words from the homily, but new, spontaneous words.

"Thank God for drugs!" I cried.

Stunned silence. Then 400 mouths dropped open. It's likely I was thinking that only someone on serious drugs would try a stunt like this.

Mac leaned toward me, concealing a grin with his hand.

"Mama's gonna kill you," he muttered. I glanced at Nancy. She did not look happy. Others did, though, judging by their laughter.

I looked at Blakely, as beautiful as I'd ever seen her, then back at Mac. I stepped away from the lectern and leaned in to whisper to him, placing a hand on his shoulder. Mac took my place at the lectern and began reading the homily I had written. I listened to him speak the words I had labored over and somehow I did not feel like they were my words. I did, though, feel very much like a dad – Mac's dad and Blakely's dad.

I took my seat next to Nancy. She was quiet and content, hopeful, ready for whatever would come. I thought I might spot lingering traces of murderous intent. Instead, she met my eyes and offered a watery smile and gave her gaze back first to our son, then to our daughter and then to the man who would be our daughter's husband. I kept my eyes on Nancy, on her familiar profile, and I felt her joy. I also felt the hard tug and knew she felt, too. Our little girl was now no longer little, and no longer just ours. No more. The recessional played. I turned my eyes to Buddy and Blakely and watched their backs as they took their first walk as husband and wife.

# 21

## *Shake Your Booty*

"Joe-Joe, we can play fast music, right?" my grand-daughter asked, and I nodded. Carson was three. She ran to the bedroom where Grandma Nancy – "An-Ma" – kept her CD player. It held a collection of golden old-ies. Carson's favorite was Chubby Checker's "Let's Twist Again," followed closely by The Village People's "YMCA."

"Just for a little while," I called after her. "Then we have to go."

Carson fired up the CD and pressed buttons until she found Chubby. She squealed and jumped and came down with her hips swiveling. She pumped her arms and loud-ly sang along.

*Let's twist again, like we did last summer. Let's twist again, like we did last year. Twistin' time is here.*

I stood in the doorway and watched. She squatted down low and made a production of shaking her little rear end.

"Dance, Joe-Joe, dance!" Carson hollered and waved excitedly.

I shook my head.

"Joe-Joe's too tired," I shouted over the music. "I'll just watch." I'm told most people who see me dance think I'm drunk. No sober person would willingly do what I do in public and call it dancing.

"YMCA" started.

*Young man, are you far from home? Young man, are you all alone?* Trumpets blasted and drums crashed. *You can go to the YMCA, the YMCA.* Now in her socks, Carson slid across the floor, freezing as the music paused, then jerking her arms robotically when the beat came back.

Once more she pleaded, "Joe-Joe! Dance with me!"

Again I balked. I had gloom on my mind. My son was going through a rough patch. And a good friend, whose husband had died two months earlier, had just lost her parents on the same day. So much loss. I thought of my own parents, dead for fifteen years. They would never see Carson dance.

Chubby Checker was back. Carson's tiny fingers tugged on my hand.

"Joooe-Joooe, *please*," she begged. "You have to dance. You *have* to."

She wouldn't let go, so I let her drag me to the middle of the room, where I reluctantly began doing my fractured version of The Twist. Carson clapped merrily and exploded into motion again. She wiggled her body and bobbed her head, jumping and spinning and tousling her hair.

"Joe-Joe, shake your booty! You gotta shake your booty!"

"Shake my what? My booty?"

"Your *booty*, Joe-Joe. Like *this*." She poked out her backside and wiggled it furiously.

I bent my knees a little and did my best to shake my booty.

"I don't think guys have a booty," I said. "And if we do, mine's too big to shake."

She looked at me with *that* look, the look that would not be denied. So I gave up and tried my best and fell smack on my booty. She laughed and called me silly and danced some more. I picked myself up off the floor, slipped off my shoes, and made a sideways glide Tom Cruise couldn't match.

"*Yes!*" Carson squealed.

"YMCA" was back. Carson clapped at her delight, and I did too. She stepped to her left, then to her right, and shimmied her shoulders. I did my best to follow her. Sweat popped out on my forehead and trickled down my back.

"*YMCA, YMCA,*" the Village People sang. We raised our arms high and awkwardly spelled out the letters, never getting it right or even close.

Carson bolted to one side of the room and slid back across to the other. It looked like fun so I joined her. We slid back and forth, high-fiving as we passed, catching glimpses of ourselves in the full-length mirror on the door. We looked good. I twisted downward as she rotated upward. I separated my feet and took her hands and swung her between my legs.

"Do it again Joe-Joe. Do it again!" she hollered, and I did. "Do it again Joe-Joe. Do it again!" And I did it again, a thousand times, maybe two. I wasn't counting.

We slid, twisted, laughed, and raised our hands and slid across the floor until I collapsed onto the bed. Carson was still full of vinegar and not ready to quit. She clambered up beside me, plunked her booty on my chest and gave me a curious look.

"I can't do it anymore, sweetie," I wheezed. "Joe-Joe's dyin' here."

"You're silly, Joe-Joe. Wait 'til I tell An-Ma that you danced." She slid off me, bounced to the floor, and shook her booty out the door. Carson was simply being Carson in motion, just a three-year-old having fun, reminding me of a great truth. When times are tough, when it hurts, it helps to dance.

But you have to dance to know that.

# 22

## *Marci*

Marci, an attractive forty-year-old, blue-eyed blonde, entered my office. Bipolar illness brought her here. She struggled with periods of depression and an occasional manic episode characterized by a sizable spending spree. Medication kept things in check, but psychotherapy had been needed. Before she relocated, a previous therapist referred her to me.

For years, Marci had been the administrative assistant to the president of a large corporation – his right-hand man, so to speak. I found her very pleasant (especially to look at), witty and quite opinionated. She found my comments insightful and my stories funny.

During one session she revealed that she had once worked as a prostitute. *Wow!* I thought. *What's that about?* Chuckling, I told her about my humorous experience at nineteen with the French prostitute and the chocolate naked ladies and how I thought I'd been bilked when I signed over the $50 travelers' check and got no change back. I waited for her to laugh. But this time, Marci was not amused.

"So, what exactly did the experience of embracing the bosoms of little chocolate naked ladies teach you?" Her tone was edgy. The mention of the word "bosoms" caused my eyes to glance at hers. "Quit staring, and answer my question. What did you learn?"

Embarrassed, I stumbled for a reply. "Uh . . . I don't know. It was a long time ago." Attempting to regain control I said, "My story obviously hit a painful nerve. Maybe we should explore that."

"Don't give me that counselor crap." She leaned forward. "When the prostitute gave you the box of chocolate naked ladies and you discovered your returned travelers' check, what, if anything, did you learn?"

So much for regaining control. My father's voice rattled my memory: *And why wilt thou, my son, be ravished with a strange woman?* I was feeling nineteen again. I cleared my throat and attempted a response. "Uh, well, I mainly remember feeling relieved that I got my money back." The forty-year-old memory returned with greater clarity. "I fell asleep holding the box, wishing I'd made better use of my time with her. I remember my buddy bragging about how he certainly got his money's worth." I gave a small chuckle, hoping she would join me.

"That's it? That's what you learned?" Now Marci *was* angry. Her look pressed me for more. "I was only nineteen for God's sake!" I said defensively. "What was I supposed to see? She was gorgeous. I was ravished with this strange woman! It was Paris!"

Marci did not let up. "You failed to see *her*, the woman right in front of you!" I was befuddled. She began fumbling with her purse, getting out her checkbook to pay for the counseling session. "I can see our time is up," she said. "Here." She handed me the check and left.

During lunch I could not eat, nor could I stop thinking

about what Marci said. A teachable moment registered in my mind, what one of my seminary professors called the "malady of I-Sight." After all these years, I still saw the French prostitute from my limited point of view: a strange woman whose bosoms I had failed to embrace.

Back in my office, I opened my Bible to Luke 7:36: Jesus's encounter with a prostitute. While sharing a meal at the home of Simon the Pharisee, a woman "who had lived a sinful life in that town" washed, anointed and kissed the feet of Jesus. Repelled by her behavior, Simon wondered if Jesus knew "who is touching him and what kind of woman she is. . . ."

Jesus asked Simon the same question Marci had asked me, *Do you see this woman?* No. He didn't. Maybe Marci was also wondering if I was going to see her as more than an attractive blonde with bipolar disorder.

I opened my desk drawer, took out a pen and a piece of paper, and I wrote.

"Dear Marci, with gratitude."

I folded the check Marci had written and slipped it in an envelope.

# 23

## *Baptism*

The baby monitor beside my bed squawked loudly. The digital clock read 2:22 a.m. I got my seven-month-old grandson, James Wyatt, out of his crib, changed his diaper (always a joy at 2:22 a.m.), and fed him his bottle. Nancy and I were babysitting at Blakely and Buddy's for the weekend.

James Wyatt's brown eyes and long eyelashes stared at me as if he wanted to talk. So we talked.

"You know, this time next week is a big day for you. You get baptized. And guess what? Ole Joe-Joe here is doing the honors."

The big smile he gave me was accompanied by a loud fart. Next to throwing up, James Wyatt's favorite activity was farting.

"Don't tell anyone, but I've never done a baptism, not once in thirty years as a minister. There was this one time, though, when I was concluding an evening service. This guy came forward, accepting Jesus and wanting baptism. I didn't know what to do. Nobody had ever repented when I preached."

James Wyatt blinked. I took that to mean he was curious.

"Well, I reverently placed my arm around the man's shoulder, leaned in so it would look like we were praying, and whispered in his ear, 'I just got word from the Lord. Jesus told me to tell you you're a week early. So, if you don't mind, sit back down and walk the aisle next Sunday when your pastor returns. Don't worry. You're covered, you know, in the event something happens.'

"Anyway, James Wyatt, you're my first. And guess what? I get to speak! Only for three minutes, though. Father Ken is allowing me a few – a very few – words when the ceremony is over. Besides your baptism, he's preaching on Pentecost and there's also communion. Episcopalians like to pack a lot into an hour. Any idea on how to say something profound in three minutes?"

James Wyatt was fast asleep. So I put him back in his crib, got my Bible and notepad and sat at the kitchen table, waiting for the profound. I was asleep, drooling on my notepad when dawn broke and James Wyatt's three-year-old sister, Carson, came bounding in.

"Joe-Joe, what are you doing?" She crawled up into my lap.

"Oh, just contemplating my existential anxiety," I replied.

"I don't know what sistential siety is. But we gotta watch *Wonder Pets*."

"I thought we might watch the *Law and Order* marathon. You like *Law and Order*, don't you?"

She gave me an exasperated look.

"Joe-Joe, we've talked about this before. *Log and Older* is for grownups.

"What about breakfast? Do you want a frozen waffle?"

"No. I want ice cream. I want ice cream in the pink bowl."

"Comin' up." I dropped two scoops of vanilla ice cream in the pink bowl. The privilege of being a grandparent.

As I flipped the channels hunting for *Wonder Pets,* the voice of an evangelist hollered: "And Jesus said to the young expert in the law, 'You tell me. How does the law read?' The young man replied, 'Love the Lord your God with all your heart, with all your mind, with all your soul. And your neighbor as yourself.' Jesus told him, 'Do this and you will live.'"

The evangelist looked right at me and said, "Eternal life begins by loving your neighbor as yourself. It begins with a life of compassion."

I ate my ice cream, watched *Wonder Pets* return a baby bird to its mother's nest, and thought about the words of the evangelist. Eternal life begins with a compassionate life. *That's* what I would talk about! A compassionate life.

Later that morning, Nancy fired up the vacuum cleaner. That was my cue to leave. You don't want to get in Nancy's way when she's running the vacuum cleaner. I pulled out the double-sided stroller and headed out for a peaceful stroll with Carson and James Wyatt. As we circled the block, I thought about a compassionate life. A story about Reverend David Wilkerson came to mind.

He believed God wanted him to go to New York City and preach salvation to the troubled kids who ran in street gangs. So he placed a soapbox on a street corner, stood on the box and shouted to all who would listen to accept Jesus or spend eternity in hell. One day, an angry teenager confronted Reverend Wilkerson.

"I don't care about hell! I'm already there," he shouted.

"I have no parents. I live in a rundown building. I steal food to eat. I don't even have socks and shoes to wear!"

Reverend Wilkerson looked at the kid's bare feet. He didn't know what to say. He had no words for that. Finally, he sat on his soapbox, took off his shoes and socks, gave them to the kid, and walked away. It's much easier to preach salvation than to be compassionate. That day, Reverend Wilkerson backed up his words with an act of compassion.

Good story. Maybe that's how I should use my three minutes.

Carson climbed out of the stroller, wanting to run around. She threw pebbles. She ran through the sprinkler in someone's front yard, then climbed a fence and fell.

"Owww! Joe-Joe! It stings!" Carson's knee was skinned, and I could see blood percolating to the surface. I picked her up, and she clung to my neck sobbing. Her crying made James Wyatt cry, so I picked him up, too.

"Carry me home, Joe-Joe!" Carson wailed. James Wyatt seemed to think that was a good idea for him, too. So with Carson on one side of me, James Wyatt on the other, and the stroller in front, I began the quarter-mile walk home.

"Carson," I said. "Can you loosen your grip on my neck? Joe-Joe needs to breathe." Carson let go of my neck, causing her to lurch, lose her balance and nearly fall to the ground. I jerked her back to safety, disrupting James Wyatt enough that he amped up his crying and spit-up on my shoulder. When Nancy spied us coming up the driveway, she swooped down like an angel of mercy and took Carson. This gave me an opportunity to share another story with James Wyatt, who, by then, had moved his attention to pulling on my hair with his goopy hands.

The story was about an old lady named Agnes. Years ago, as a young Catholic nun, she went to India, determined to make sure the hungry kids there got enough to eat and drink. As many nuns do, she eventually took another name. Teresa. The people of India loved her and called her Mother Teresa.

I recalled for James Wyatt the time she spoke at a conference on science and religion led by a group of quantum physicists. The head physicist introduced her as someone who had endured many hardships to help not only the poor people of India but many others in need around the world. For her many great deeds she was awarded the Nobel Peace Prize. Mother Teresa surprised the large gathering of physicists when she said, "We can do no great things. Only many small things with great love, and for that you sometimes receive the greatest gift of all: 'thank you.'"

I carried James Wyatt into the family room to check on Nancy and Carson, who proudly showed off her Minnie Mouse band-aid. "Joe-Joe, let's go 'splorin'."

I was pretty sure she was kidding, so I laughed and said, "Now that's a really terrific idea." Next thing I knew, Carson's hand was in my hand, and Nancy was holding James Wyatt.

"Have a nice time," she said.

Carson headed us in the direction of the elementary school playground not far away.

"How's your sistential siety?" Carson asked.

"It's pretty bad. You and James Wyatt have worn me out. Maybe we should sit quietly in the shade and meditate deeply upon our navels."

"You're silly, Joe-Joe."

"You know about navels, don't you?" I tickled hers. "You press them hard enough and your butt falls off."

"Joe-Joe, you're not supposed to say 'butt.' I'm gonna tell An-ma."

Time to bargain. Carson pointed toward the trio of swings in the playground. "I like to go high, Joe-Joe. Super high." As I was gearing up to secure my side of the bargain, Carson skipped off toward the swings, yelling at me to "hurry up, Joe-Joe!"

I ran to keep up with her. By the time I got there, I was holding my side. "Carson," I said, out of breath. "Let's look in the windows." No sense admitting to her that her grandpa was out of shape. Carson stopped abruptly and chirped, "Okay." Pretty clever of me. And so I held her up to the window, we both peered in, and I readied myself for a wave of nostalgia.

I saw a Smartboard instead of a chalkboard, computers instead of pencil holders. There were no alphabet letters strung around the classroom or tidy rows of desks. Instead, chairs were arranged in a half-circle focused on the Smartboard. So much for nostalgia. I was just about to say something to Carson when I spied something familiar: Winnie the Pooh and Piglet painted on the wall.

"Let's go swing," Carson said, squirming to get down. She hit the ground running and by the time I got to her, she was already in the swing, pumping her legs. She squealed when I gave her a push.

"Higher, Joe-Joe, higher!"

It seemed to me she was as high as she needed to be, so I caught the swing seat instead and held her aloft, making Carson hold tight to the chains. "Lemme go, Joe-Joe. Lemme go!" When I let her go, she kicked out her legs in front of her, building her own momentum. We got into a rhythm: me catching, holding and letting go. Carson pumping, kicking, lifting her legs and feet. As we did, I thought about Winnie the Pooh and Piglet walking down a long, lonely road. By the end of the day they were tired, so they stopped to rest and soon they fell asleep. After a while, it got dark. As it did, Piglet had a dream, and the dream woke him up. Scared, Piglet ran around in the dark, calling for Pooh Bear. His shouts woke Pooh Bear, who was also scared and ran around calling for Piglet. Then *whomp!*

"Pooh?" said Piglet, rubbing his head. "Is that you?"

"Yes! Piglet! Yes, it's me! Are you okay?" Then he hugged Piglet so tightly he could hardly breathe.

"I had a bad dream," Piglet said. "I thought I'd lost you."

The next morning they continued their journey. As they walked, Piglet sidled up to Pooh from behind.

"Pooh?" whispered Piglet.

"Yes?"

"Oh, nothing," Piglet said, taking Pooh's paw. "I just needed to know you were close by."

*That's* my three minutes, I thought. That's the story. Compassion is about having someone we love close by when we feel afraid. My existential anxiety was now relieved. I returned my focus to Carson, who, I realized, was singing now.

The next Sunday we stood together at the baptismal font. Father Ken was beside me reading the baptismal liturgy. Blakely stood in front of me, holding James Wyatt all decked out in his baptismal gown. Buddy, his father, was beside them. The rest of our family formed a semicircle. Father Ken completed the readings. Blakely handed me James Wyatt. With my lips pressed against his ear, I secretly whispered, "Please don't fart or throw up." Sucking his pacifier, he batted his long eyelashes. I dipped my hand into the bowl of water three times.

"James Wyatt Arthur, I baptize you in the name of the Father, the Son and the Holy Ghost. Amen."

Father Ken looked at me. The clock was running. In the end, none of the three stories touched me as much as the experience I had with Carson that Sunday afternoon at the swings. I turned to face the congregation, James Wyatt in my arms.

"James Wyatt, it doesn't really matter what our path in life is. What's important is that we walk that path with compassion. Jesus led a compassionate life. Stare hard at him, James Wyatt. There will be times when life scares you. There will be times when doing small things goes unnoticed. You will get tired and feel like giving up. And there will be times when loving brings you sorrow, and you look to Jesus for relief but the fear, the tiredness and the sadness won't go away. During those times remember this story:

"Last Sunday afternoon I was pushing your sister Carson in a swing. As I pushed her, she sang.

*Jesus love me, this I know,*
*For the Bible tells me so.*
*Yes, Jesus love me. Yes, Jesus love me.*
*Yes, Jesus love me, for the Bible tells me so.*

"The harder she pumped, the louder she sang. I asked Carson, 'Who is Jesus?'

"In her matter-of-fact tone, she said, 'I don't know . . . but he love me.'

"So, James Wyatt, when you can't find Jesus, *sing.* Sing the song and know that no matter how difficult life gets, Jesus found you first, and Jesus will never let you go."

I kissed him and handed him back to his mother. Right on cue, the choir sang.

*Jesus loves me, this I know,*
*For the Bible tells me so.*
*Yes, Jesus loves me. Yes, Jesus loves me.*
*Yes, Jesus loves me, for the Bible tells me so.*